Life Is Complicated:

My journey with Asperger Syndrome

Barry John Evans

ISBN-13:
978-1507778272

ISBN-10:
1507778279

Dedication

I would like to dedicate this book to anyone who has been supportive to me over the years through my struggles and to those who have always been there for me, especially my mum.

I would also like to dedicate this book to anyone who can relate to it and hopefully gain something positive from reading it.

Contents

Chapter 1: Welcome To My World

First of all, thank you to those who are reading this. I decided that after my 1st book (A New ME: an autobiography focusing mainly on my struggle with the illness Myalgic Encephalomyelitis) that I would write another book on what life is like living with Asperger Syndrome. A lot of people have asked me through social media what it's been like growing up with the condition, mainly mums who have children who have been through similar experiences to me. I felt it would be beneficial to write this because a) I find it easier to express myself through writing as opposed to personal contact and b) I hope it will help those struggling with the condition and also those who care for people with Aspergers.

(A New ME published in June 2014)

What Is Asperger Syndrome?

Rather than give you a 2 page essay of explaining what the condition is, I'm going to give you a very short paragraph taken from the website **www.autism.org.uk**. Firstly, this is because you'll get a better idea as you read on without me explaining what it is. Secondly, I'm not the best person at explaining things simply...

I often like writing numerical symbols rather than the actual words. This seems more logical to me. As was the case with my last book, I am going to donate 10% of all profits made to charity. I have chosen the previously mentioned website to donate to as I feel it gives a very good description of what Asperger Syndrome actually is. They also do a lot of good work for the cause.

So here we go:

"Asperger syndrome is a form of **autism**, *which is a lifelong disability that affects how a person makes sense of the world, processes information and relates to other people. Autism is often described as a 'spectrum disorder' because the condition affects*

people in many different ways and to varying degrees".
(Taken from www.autism.org.uk)

Now you have a very brief idea of what the condition involves, I'm going to tell you about the thought processes I went through in deciding to write this book. Why? It shows certain autistic traits that you will come to recognize throughout the book. Some of it may seem crazy at first but you will start to see a pattern forming as the book goes on...

Formatting The Book

I found it incredibly difficult thinking of the right format for this book. I'd decided on at least 5 different ways I could lay it out. I like to work from a set list so decided to search through different websites explaining what Asperger Syndrome is whilst using the key areas mentioned as different chapters.

I always have to have my 1st chapter explaining what the book is about and the last chapter as a conclusion because I like a beginning and an end. I dislike open endings. Even though I like to think I have an open mind, I find certain things have to be in black and white. Take for example the pictures in this book: they're black and white too, but not in the same sort of black and white as mentioned above. Black and white stands out to me as professional, not only that but it costs less money when it comes to printing. I have a multitasking mind.

Back to open endings, well, they give me headaches. I like to know exactly where I stand however blunt the answer may be. I don't like not knowing things. This can be my downfall as it can come across as impatient and certain issues are pushed before they should be.

This is a prime example of how I can go off the original subject. My teachers at school, college and university all said the same thing. I produced good work but I tended to wander off the subject and talk about something irrelevant. Always refer to the initial question they would say. I'm meant to be explaining how I came to format my book and now I've ended up talking about being open minded. You will see this the more I talk. You'll also notice that I don't use any exclamation marks; I feel that this shows my lack of expression and my struggle with raising or lowering the tone of my voice which will be explained later on. I can also be pretty intense too, unintentionally.

Anyway, I thought maybe I could divide the book into 5 chapters: a beginning and an end, whilst the 3 chapters in the middle would focus on the main areas of Asperger Syndrome: 'Social Communication', 'Social Interaction' and 'Social Imagination'. This should have worked well because 5 is a number I like. It's like with the car radio and my stereo, the volume has to be on a multiple of 5. Sometimes this can result in the music being slightly too loud or slightly too quiet but that's a sacrifice I'm willing to make.

What was wrong with this format? Well the 3 chapters in the middle weren't specific enough, I'd made a list of all the things to mention in the book and I was having difficulty in deciding which section to put them in. I didn't want it to be too formal either with a book full of bullet points. Why is it called a bullet point because it doesn't really look like a bullet does it? It could just be called a ball point or even a circle point. I don't like pointy things either because they're sharp. Things like this are things I have learned not to share with people, but seeing as I'm letting you all explore my mind I will mention every little detail whilst trying not to be too tedious.

I like to get my thoughts out onto paper and very rarely edit what I've written bar the odd spelling mistake of course and maybe the layout of a few paragraphs. I could always have got a ghost writer to help me out but I don't think that would show you what I'm trying to share with you in this book. Certain things may seem disjointed but then my mind is a little disjointed at times. Doing it this way shows you a true representation of me and how my mind actually works.

I had trouble in school finding the differences between a report and a newspaper article however many times the teachers explained it to me and to this day have trouble differentiating between things that others may think are simple. I sometimes feel the need to repeat myself too because my mind finds it hard to switch quickly to another subject. I apologize if I start to sound a little repetitive.

Anyway, so the idea of 5 chapters didn't quite work despite it being a good number so I thought of something slightly more specific like having 2 chapters in the middle of a beginning and an end called 'Problems with Social Interaction and Communcation' and 'Restricted and Repetetive Patterns of Thought, Interests and Physical Behaviours' (long sentence, catch your breath).

Well for a start the 2 chapters would be incredibly long and having 4 chapters doesn't sit well with me. What significance does the number 4 have? I love numbers, but not the number 4. Number 1 is sole, number 2 is a couple, all things come in 3's, 5 is a multiple of 5, but 4, I don't have any connection with that number whatsoever unless it's on the back of a football shirt because 4 is a defenders number and I used to wear that number before somebody else took it, then I didn't want to wear it again so I took the number 5 shirt. I'm not very keen on the number 6, but at least you can get 2 multiples of 3 out of it, but then I prefer 9 because that means 3 multiples of 3: despite that, number 9 always has to be rounded to 10 to make it whole. Number 7 is considered a lucky number and number 8 is a special number. Always first on a lottery ticket when I rarely get one. I don't really know why I like the number 8 but I do. My only early memory of that number is when I think of the Mr Men books. I loved the Mr Men and had the whole set. They all had numbers which made them a lot more exciting. Forget about the inside content, the numbers on the spine of the book will do just fine. I liked Mr Messy and he was number 8. It could also be the fact that the number 8 is my birthday number. It's also symmetrical; it's like 2 footballs 1 on top of the other. I will talk about symmetry later on in the 'Special Interests' section.

Back to the format, I thought I'd found 1 I liked. It meant there would be 7 chapters (lucky number). These chapters would be 'Problems with Social Skills', 'Restricted or 'Repetitive Behaviours', 'Unusual Preoccupations', 'Communication Difficulties', 'Limited Range of Interests', 'Coordination Problems', 'Skilled or Talented'. Well for starters I can't do a chapter on 'Skilled or Talented' as that would be extremely arrogant and conceited of me. I can't stand arrogant people, especially when they've got nothing to be arrogant about. Also, having 7 chapters sounds good, but I forgot about the beginning and end so then it would be 9 chapters. When it's 9 I have to round it to 10 but I can't change any of the chapters because I got them from a set list of symptoms. I also found it difficult to differentiate between 'Problems with Social Skills' and 'Communication Difficulties'.

The amount of needless stress this has caused me is ridiculous; I've probably spent longer deciding on the format than actually writing the book. I'm not happy about this but I'm just going to have to format it as I go along. I will start off chronologically and anything very specific and relevant I write about will be made into a chapter. You can guarantee that by time I've finished writing that the book will consist of 5, 7, 8 or 10 chapters. Having 3 chapters wouldn't be enough and once it's gone past 10 I have to start going in multiples of 5 and 15 chapters would be too many, but having said that there may well end up being 15 chapters in this book...

Doing it this way means that it's more free flowing and not as robotic. After all, everyone with Asperger Syndrome is different so it wouldn't be very original of me to follow a text book and try to fit my experiences into different categories.

You may find that in parts I waffle a little but that's a true reflection of what's going on inside my mind, lots and lots...

The Final Decision

I was going to end the chapter there but I've decided to come back to it, I just couldn't work without a set list of chapters. It wasn't specific enough; I didn't know where to put what. I have a new idea though, it will involve lots of photos which will be good because it means I can write about the pictures as I go along which will recreate more memories for me. I like to do things in order too so it's a little distracting as the 2nd chapter in this book won't be written by me. It's going to be written by my mum and she'll be talking about the diagnosis process I went through. She remembers that period a lot better than I do as I was only very young. I think it will also be good to get a different perspective from someone other than myself.

I feel this is a good ending point for the chapter now. I hope you enjoy this book and gain something positive from it. I'm a little bit embarrassed by some of the content but if other people can relate to it then that's good enough for me if it helps them. I'm not crazy, just different and, at times, a little bit creative.

Chapter 2: The Diagnosis Process

Barry was born on 8th April 1991. He arrived 6
weeks early and took us somewhat by surprise! He
weighed just 5lbs and spent 2 weeks in the special
care unit at the local maternity hospital. He actually
lost weight whilst in hospital and weighed just 4lb
12 and a half oz when we arrived home. For the first
6 weeks, he slept most of the time which is typical of
premature babies. As they reach the date they were
due to arrive, they change somewhat! He was a fairly
easy baby with no particular problems. He didn't sit
up on his own until he was 8 months old and didn't
start to walk unaided until he was 16 months of age.
He had check-ups at the hospital throughout this
time due to him being premature. Any delays in
development were put down to his somewhat early
arrival so there were no particular concerns but his
speech development was very late and we started to
become slightly concerned.

From around him turning 2 years of age, we
attended local mums and toddler groups. Barry
didn't seem to actually want to interact with the

other children but would play alongside them. When it came to story time, trying to get him to sit on the mat with the others was almost impossible! He couldn't seem to sit still for more than a minute... if that! I used to feel my heart sinking as story time was announced. Let the battle commence! One of the groups was a local church group. It was run by the most lovely people. We didn't attend the church services at this time but we did start to go quite a few years later. We went on to become members and remain a part of our church family. They have been a tremendous support to us over the years and we have so much to be thankful for.

Speech Therapy

As there was a delay in speech development, Barry was referred to a Speech Therapist at the Children's Centre. The lady we saw was lovely; however I remember feeling somewhat anxious before our appointments as the same old problem happened... the battle to stop Barry from doing anything except sitting down! He would be running around the room, crawling under the desk and rolling around, anything except sitting on the chair! She used to loan us toys and games to take home which would hopefully encourage speech. He was happy to play with them, but development was still slow. She suggested that we should start seeing someone who was a pre-school advisor as he approached 3 years old. This was a turning point for us, particularly myself. The pre-school advisor visited us at home. I looked forward to her visits. She was very friendly and approachable. I was able to share all my concerns with her and she was able to see what Barry was like in his home environment. I remember her asking me on her first visit to describe the problems as I saw them. We discussed his level of understanding of speech and I said that I felt that he did understand when I was talking to him, but over the next few visits, I realised just how wrong I was. Guilt kicked in. Why did I not realise that my son didn't just have slow speech development? The fact was that he couldn't take in and understand what I was trying to convey to him. I was his mum. Why didn't I understand him better?

Pre-School Advisor

The pre-school advisor was brilliant. Understanding what the problems are is the first step to learning how to face them and deal with things. Barry had started attending a local playgroup by now. She went along to observe from a distance to see how he was coping and behaving in a social situation on his own. He had always found mixing socially quite hard and at playgroup he kept himself to himself quite a bit and joined in from a distance rather than being in the middle of things. It was decided that a place at the local authority nursery would benefit him. There was a waiting list, but at least he was on it. Fortunately, the wait wasn't too long after all, probably only a few weeks. He went along there for a couple of sessions each week. The matron and staff were very nice and really understood the problems, which they were obviously used to encountering. He attended this nursery right up until he started at his first Primary School. The school had their own nursery so he started there when he was 4 and a half years old.

The year in the school nursery class went smoothly. He seemed to fit in well although he was still reluctant to get involved sometimes. His speech started to slowly develop which was a relief. All in all, it was a good year. After the summer holidays, he started in the reception class. Seeing him go in in his smart uniform brought a lump to my throat, like most mums! I was worried how he would cope with this new stage in his life. A few weeks into the term, our new baby arrived. Barry was delighted to have a little brother. When his teacher asked the class to bring in something that was special to them to show the rest of the class, he insisted on taking Sean! I explained she meant maybe a favourite toy or belonging, but he was adamant. "She said something special and that's what he is!" So in he went. It was lovely as the rest of the class gathered round to greet him!

Starting School

As the rest of the year passed, he made a few new friends and seemed to progress well. His Maths work was very good and to this day is something he is very good at. His reading was coming along nicely too. It was when he started in year 1 that worries again crept in. His ability to concentrate wasn't good and the teacher told us that at times he seemed to just 'go blank' and she had to say his name a few times to get his attention. At this time, we were referred to an Epilepsy Specialist. Although he had never had any fits or anything like that, they wanted to investigate whether these moments when he appeared to 'go blank' could be linked in any way to this area. He attended a few appointments but the specialist we saw then told us that although it was clear there were problems, she didn't feel there was any link to any form of Epilepsy, so we were discharged from that clinic.

Changing School

Towards the end of the first term in year 2, changes were happening. We were moving house in the New Year. Unfortunately, though we were only moving to the other side of town, this meant a change of school for Barry. So after Christmas, he started at a new primary school. He coped with the change reasonably well. We hadn't been able to get him into our first choice of school, looking back though; I believe things happen for a reason. His new teacher was a very nice lady and he seemed to settle in and make friends. The same problems were still there though. Lack of concentration, difficulty taking in information and processing it, and sometimes seeming to 'switch off'. If he was told, for example, to hang his coat up, put his bag over there and sit down at the table, he would just stand there looking confused and actually do nothing. Yet if he was told to do these things one by one he had no problem at all. He was on the 'special needs' register at school and we had regular feedback from the teachers.

Finding A Breakthrough

During a meeting with his class teacher, she asked us if anyone we had ever seen about Barry had ever mentioned the condition 'Asperger Syndrome'. They hadn't. In fact, we had never heard of it. Apparently his teacher's niece had been diagnosed with this and she said that a lot of the concerns with regard to Barry were very similar. After our chat, I read up a lot about it and felt that what I was reading described my son very well! This turned out to be a real breakthrough.

I made an appointment with Barry's GP and told him about this meeting, what his teacher had said, and about the stuff I had read and how I felt it described Barry so well. A comment was made about how teachers were there to teach and not diagnose medical conditions! Despite this, I asked for a referral to a psychologist at The Children's Centre. I was adamant. The doctor agreed to refer him, despite stating that in his opinion reading articles was not the way to get to the root of the problem. I stuck to my guns, whilst being made to feel that I was a somewhat neurotic mum. I was told we would possibly have to wait several months for an appointment, but it was better than nothing. So we waited.

One day, a few months later, the telephone rang at home. The man introduced himself; he was the psychologist at the Children's Centre who was dealing with the referral. He sounded very pleasant but a little confused as to the reason for the referral. Apparently it had been made clear that I had initiated the referral despite the GP's doubts. I explained why I felt like this and told him that I really would like him to reassure me that Barry didn't in fact have Aspergers! Unfortunately this wasn't to be the case.

During this period, another change of school took place. As I said previously, when we moved house, we hadn't been able to get Barry into the school of our choice. We appealed against this decision and a year later, a term into year 3, a place became available which we accepted. I look back at that decision now as being a big mistake. He had settled at the other school, and we had made a lot of progress in our search for answers. This next move proved to be a negative one for him. Halfway through school it is more difficult to make friends as others have established groups of peers. He was unsettled at the new school, but I had no idea how unhappy he really was.

Our progress with the psychologist was positive. Over the next few months we met regularly with him and another lady at the centre. Sometimes the whole family went along, and they also saw Barry on his own. Barry and his brother would be given lots of paper, pencils and crayons to draw whatever they wanted, also a wide variety of toys which was all part of the assessment process.

Eventually, after approximately 6 months of appointments and assessments, we had a meeting with the doctor and he told us that in his view Barry had Asperger Syndrome. I remember that day so well. It was a real mixture of feelings and emotions. There was a huge sense of relief that after all the years of acknowledging that there was a problem, but never actually knowing what it was exactly, now we knew. There was also sadness though. The worry of how my son would cope with life as he grew up. As a parent, we all worry about our children and want them to have as few problems as possible. The diagnosis opened the door to all sorts of new worries and concerns. But at least we knew what we were dealing with now and he could have the right kind of help and support.

We told his school and they were very good. Appropriate support during lessons was set up. A lot of these difficulties though came from the other children though. Other kids always notice when someone is slightly 'different'. School playgrounds can be very harsh places and sadly break time was Barry's least favourite time of the day. He was bullied and didn't really make any good friendships. The school did their best to deal with any issues we brought up but can't be everywhere all the time.

Group

During this period of time, Barry was invited along to a group run by the psychologist's co-worker. He went once a week at the centre after school for 6 weeks. It was a small group of boys who had similar problems to Barry. He was nervous at first but then found he really enjoyed going! They would do various activities each week. One session, they all helped to write a story about a boy starting at a new school and how he felt about the whole situation. Reading it afterwards was very interesting indeed, and very revealing. Another project was building a roller coaster out of newspaper! It took a while, but they got there... and it stood upright! They were very proud of themselves. This was to encourage teamwork and co-operation, and it worked very well! They all really enjoyed themselves. All in all, this group was a very positive experience for Barry.

Conclusion

As he moved on through his time at school, Barry learnt how to deal with things a lot better. He was good at covering things up though. I didn't realise just how unhappy he was throughout his time at Primary School. Looking back now, I feel so sad that he struggled so much and guilty that I didn't know all that was going on. I so wish he had felt more able to confide in me.

Things have improved so much for him over the years though. He has grown into a lovely young man who has a very good understanding of his condition. He has developed coping strategies, as he explains here in this book. He is also constantly working on trying to overcome his limitations. I have so much respect and admiration for my son.

The Question

I know that somewhere in this book Barry is going to include a Q & A section. I thought I would like to ask him a question myself. While he has been writing this, we have had numerous long conversations over a never ending supply of coffee! It has given me much more insight into what is actually going on inside his head... continually. My question to my son is this:

"Are you able to ever completely switch off, relax, and just think about nothing in particular? If so, for how long?"

I think I have a new understanding of just how hard his mind is working almost all of the time. As well as having Asperger Syndrome, he was diagnosed with M.E. 2 years ago. His strength of character and a living faith in God are what get him through life. I have so much respect for him.

This chapter was written by one extremely proud mum x

Chapter 3: School Shenanigans

I want to make sure that this chapter gets across my autistic traits rather than focusing on bullying as it may seem that way because bullying was a massive part of my school life. The bullying made my autistic traits much worse and I have no doubt that if more understanding people had been around me, my childhood would have been greatly improved. I didn't like reliving this period in my life but it's significant to this book. I think this chapter would fit best here as I will be talking about the time just after I was diagnosed. People would always say to me that your school years are always your best but in my eyes they couldn't have been more wrong. The only positive I gained from school is that I'd hated it so much that it meant my later years could only be better.

Am I A Vegetable?

It wasn't until the year after the diagnosis that I knew anything about Asperger Syndrome. It always reminds me of the vegetable asparagus because both words start with 'asp'.

Anyway, the day I was told I had 'Asparagus Syndrome' I remember very well. It was a Sunday afternoon and I had some English homework to complete for the following day. I always struggled with homework because there were no teachers there to tell me what to do and I was always too afraid to ask for help in class. I'd been pleading with my mum for a few hours to help me with my homework. That was when she told me about my diagnosis and what it meant. I felt a bit better after that knowing there was a reason why I couldn't understand my homework as easily as others seemed to, even though I didn't really understand what Aspergers was until a lot later on. I was still wary asking for help mainly because my peers would wonder why I was having extra support and I didn't want to stand out any more than I already did. I mean, could you imagine James Bond or Action Man sitting in class asking for help? Even though I didn't like them, they were cool and very popular, and I wanted to be cool too.

"Friends"

Before talking about the boring side of school like lessons and teachers, I'm going to talk about my difficulties in other areas, whilst trying to keep it as chronological as possible for the first part, starting with friends.

Making friends at school was extremely hard, particularly after I'd joined my 3rd Primary School in 1999. "Friends" took advantage of me as they knew I was vulnerable. I was the kid who was the easy target. I was a very quiet person: it started due to a fear of saying the wrongs things. I was used to people making fun of me for saying inappropriate things so I decided it was best to not say anything at all. That way there would be less chance of me being made a mockery of... but then I was bullied for being quiet anyway. I would say more in 5 minutes when I got home than in a whole day at school. Any anger vented up would be taken out on my mum because she was never horrible to me and I couldn't stand up to people who were horrible.

A so called "friend" came round for tea once only to reveal the next day he only came round so he could see what Playstation games I had. I loved playing on the Playstation and even had my favourite game stolen from me by a neighbour. I was always very loyal to my friends so things like this hurt, a lot. My parents bought me the same game new, but it wasn't the same because the sticker on the front was different and I didn't like that.

I would talk about wrestling (my early school intensive interest) to my so called "friends" and be confused when no-one showed an interest. I took it personally because I'd spent so long the night before thinking of the questions I was going to ask the next day.

It was always a struggle to know when a friendship was real or not as I had a very poor understanding of body language and whether people were being serious or not. I don't want to give too much away as I'll be explaining a lot more about my social difficulties later on.

Ice Cream Saga

Going round to someone's house after school was much more relaxed, they would act differently. I only had to worry about communication with them and if I said the wrong thing then only they would know about it. Being given ice cream with a spoon already in the bowl was my nightmare. It made it impossible for me to examine the spoon because it had ice cream on it. That spoon could have dirt on but the ice cream would cover it up. I made sure I would make as little contact between the spoon and my mouth as possible. I didn't enjoy it at all. It was also a nightmare being given a drink with marks around the rim. I tried to hide the fact I was cleaning it with my fingers before I drank. If the water splashed up to the rim I couldn't tell, that's why I didn't like fizzy pop, it was unpredictable. I would make as little contact as possible and feel the need to wash my mouth afterwards several times.

Ronald McDonald-Gate

At school I had to have a packed lunch, I had to know where the food had come from. When I first went to high school I got a free pass for school meals but I wouldn't use it because I couldn't understand the menu. I didn't like it when others sat close to me because they might breathe on my food and then I'd find it hard to eat. I didn't want other people's germs on my food. If they laughed then an unidentifiable substance might fly out of their mouths. I have a vivid memory at a birthday party at McDonald's where, after I blew out the candles, a little bit of spit flew out of someone's straw when they were messing about and onto Ronald McDonald on the centre of my birthday cake. I had my eye fixated on that piece begging inside my head that I wouldn't be given that piece. Luckily, I didn't get that piece. It's just as well because I remember the name of the culprit though I won't publish it here in case something was to happen to them. I don't care if I was only 5, it would have ruined my whole birthday. McDonald's was the best thing in the world at that time, there was honestly no better thing in life at that time than going to McDonald's, no question about it.

Silly Games

I think we've pretty much covered the subject of talking about my peers so let's move onto games...

I would join in with pretend games in the playground though I never really understood the rules of them. Not only that, but they were just really bad and not very exciting. Someone came up with a game called 'Blocky' once... they could've at least come up with something original. "Army" was a popular one, pretending to shoot each other with pretend guns. I didn't understand why people would want to do this. I found it hard to imagine because it wasn't real. Using my fingers as a gun with the thumb acting as a trigger shouting "bang, you're dead" didn't really get my adrenaline going that much. At least with a game like 'Tig' you didn't have to pretend, it was all very real... though I soon got bored when I realised the rules were always changed so I was 'it'. There was another game called 'Bulldog' which in parts was quite enjoyable even though I was always the one chasing. I didn't understand why it was called what it was. It was something I would dwell on; it didn't make sense to me. There was no bulldog involved. Am I meant to be a bulldog because I'm chasing someone? But bulldogs don't typically chase people unless you hurt them or they're protecting their territory. People who were made 'it' generally weren't very popular so that meant I wasn't very popular. I didn't like that because I wanted everyone to like me. I didn't like knowing that people didn't like me; it made me think I'd done something wrong and they had the wrong impression of me. 'Manhunt' was another very popular game which was quite enjoyable. One thing that really grated on me though was that in Primary School, when you caught someone, you had to say "123 Manhunt" whereas in high school it was the other way round. I only believed the game could be played one way so didn't like it after that. I didn't like getting my uniform dirty either, I was quite considerate because the first thought that always came into my head was the cost and how my mum had bought it for me despite not having much money.

Although it wasn't a game, I enjoyed cycling. I was a very quick learner when it came to things like that and had found a new hobby. It was the same with rollerblading and ice skating too; I seemed to learn physical activities a lot quicker than academic ones, ones that are realistic of course.

Cycling Nightmare

I did my cycling proficiency in primary school. I'd passed it all ok. It was great because it meant I got to skip certain lessons each week whilst doing something I quite enjoyed.

However, the morning after I'd passed I rode my bike to school. I was confused as to why all the cars were beeping me. I was cycling on the wrong side of the road but didn't twig on to the fact that cars were coming at me from the opposite direction. I did all the difficult stuff but the most basic thing I hadn't grasped. I told a friend and they told me why I was being beeped at, it could have been that or the fact that when I rode home with them afterwards, they wondered why I was on the opposite side of the road. It didn't really make sense to me. Surely it would be better if you could see cars coming at you rather than knowing they're behind but not being able to see them? What if the wind blows them my way and they crash? If I can see a car in front of me then I know if something like that will happen. It's like a lot of things with Aspergers: at times I can find the most complicated of tasks fairly simple whereas what would appear as the most simple of tasks to others would appear difficult to me.

Bullying

As mentioned before, bullying played a big part when it came to school, mainly in primary school but it never fully stopped later on.

It got to the point where I was scared to run because people made fun of the way I did it, I would deliberately not do my best when it came to sports day because I wanted to blend in with everyone else and didn't want to stand out. It's the only reason I never took up running when I was younger, I was too self conscious of how I looked when I ran. If I didn't run then no-one could make fun out of the way I did it.

There was the daily verbal abuse but I never really got used to that. I planned ways to hide away in certain situations to lower the chance of having something horrible said about me.

Thankfully the bullying was only physical on 2 separate occasions; there were more if you included being punched as a 'joke' or these days what would be deemed as 'banter'. There was an occasion where I was dragged all over the school playground, into the toilets and into the bushes round the back. There was barbed wire near the trees. I was with a friend and the bullies put it around his neck and made threats. I didn't understand why they were doing this. I was later pleaded with not to tell the teachers because they wanted to go on a school trip. I was scared to say anything and no-one else knows about it to this day except those reading this book.

Years later I saw the person at a party. No-one had ever sucked up to me so much. They were praising me for how well I was doing at college etc. I couldn't forget what had happened in the past so I just bit my tongue and gave them a very wide berth. Some people would say that others can be very selfish but I try to see the good in everyone. I knew they could be nice so I couldn't get my head around why they would be nasty when there was no reason to be. It doesn't occur to me that some people are just like that.

On another occasion I was punched in the face on the school field for no apparent reason. Another kid said I needed to fight back but I couldn't. I didn't understand why someone would do that. I knew in my head I would stand a good chance against this person, but what if I slipped and fell over? What if I missed when I punched? Why does this have to happen to me because it makes me look weak and I don't want to look weak? I could probably have been battered and still wouldn't have fought back, that's how weak I was mentally. There was no provoking involved and I walked away trying to control the tear in my eye. I've learned how to control tears. I haven't physically cried since primary school. When there's a possibility I may shed a tear, I will channel my mind onto something different. I was always scared to show my feelings and it has stuck. I felt like I couldn't express myself as it's a sign of weakness. I would rather lock myself away in a room.

I couldn't even walk to school at one point without getting bullied. A group of 3 lads with a ring leader who attended a local high school would physically stop me from walking to school each day, threaten me and make me feel the size of a pea, or even a flea. He had the face only a mother could love but I couldn't exactly tell him that could I? My dad walked to school with me one day and that put a stop to it. Nothing physical, but I couldn't fight my own battles. I was only in primary school mind so I couldn't really have been expected to. The head teacher soon found out and I had a written apology from the culprit though somehow, the head teacher had managed to lose this written apology. How can people lose things like that? All I could do was to glare at his bald shiny head in disbelief and think of an egg that was ready to hatch, which makes me think of Easter, but I'm not sure how close to Easter that incident was. I can't remember if I actually did think that but I thought it would add a little humour to a dull sub-heading.

Even outside my own home after school when I was riding my bike, someone kicked a ball which caused me to fall off. It fractured my arm. I didn't understand why they were laughing at something pretty serious. Some people get their kicks from things like that, or could it be the fact that my arm looked like a floppy sausage? My arm was in a sling for a while after that, so not very floppy as it couldn't move about. I was just gutted it wasn't my right arm because that would've given me an excuse not to take notes from the board at school.

I didn't understand how these people could carry on as normal after it had happened. No apology or remorse. If I had hurt someone even accidentally I would dwell on it day and night until I did something about it. I couldn't bear the thought of upsetting someone else. I knew how much it affected me and didn't want anyone else to feel the same.

High School

Before going into the main contents of what high school involved, I think that the first day just sums up my total lack of co-ordination. This will be spoken about in detail further on.

I remember the day pretty well actually. I started the morning off watching Kane vs Kurt Angle on my WrestleMania X8 DVD. I loved wrestling and it helped take my attention away from a daunting first day which I'd been dreading for a while.

From what I can remember, the first day went ok other than the journey home. There were very simple instructions to follow. I got the bus home but somehow managed to turn up at home 2 hours late. I even got off at the right stop. All I had to do was walk in a straight line and cross the road. My sense of direction was so bad that I couldn't find my way; the traffic and different turnings threw me. There's a turning to the right so should I go there? I know I was told to go in a straight line but the road isn't 100% straight meaning I might have to go a bit to the left? Anyway, it took me 2 hours. For a while after that my mum had to meet me at the bus stop with Katy (our dog who's still with us now 13 years later). There were school buses too but because they got so cramped, noisy and busy, I couldn't cope with them, despite it being cheaper than the regular buses.

I worked it all out in the end, but for the last few years I spent there I would walk to school and back despite it taking around 40 minutes each way.

For the first few years of high school, I would hang out with those that many would deem as the popular lads at lunch time. After a few years had passed, I got to the point where I wasn't bothered whether I was popular or not because I didn't fit in. I wasn't comfortable and didn't enjoy it. There were a select few I didn't like and I tried to avoid them. I'd put up with people like this for many years previously and decided I wanted a new direction.

The bullying wasn't as frequent as in primary school but life still wasn't pleasant. As I started to grow up, I became a lot more conscious of how I was coming across to other people. I would study the way others would act in different situations and try to implement some of these actions into my own behaviour. Sometimes it would work and other times people would wonder what on earth I was doing.

A couple of examples of this would be something as

ridiculous as someone who wore glasses squinting every time they looked up at the clock. At the time, I believed this was acceptable behaviour in that particular situation so I started to do it. A friend asked me why I did it so I soon stopped and realised it was unnecessary.

Another example of trying to use acceptable behaviour would be nodding whenever someone acknowledged me. It took me a while to grasp but I went the other way and started doing it all the time like a nodding dog. I was lucky I didn't get whiplash. Eventually, I managed to find an even balance of how much I should nod at people as a form of acknowledgement. My awareness to my behaviour was probably a main reason as to why the bullying wasn't as frequent as it was before.

One thing I found difficult when trying to understand others behaviour was understanding certain terms and phrases.

An example of this would be the term "sound" or "buzzing", I wondered what it had to do with music. Nothing actually. Sound meant ok and buzzing meant great. Even now I ask myself how these terms came about. There were jokes too which followed a particular theme. The best ones were the mum jokes; they were a regular occurrence at school and became ridiculous. My personal favourite was "Your mum on toast". Just why?

After a few years, I started hanging out with a new group who I got on with better, I wasn't bothered what others thought and just hoped nobody questioned me.

When it came to the last couple of years, I tried to skive as much as possible, I hated it so much. I'd become a bit of a loner for the most part. I actually dreaded lunch times more than the lessons. I'd figured out the longest routes around school to help get through the breaks. If I walked a certain way twice then that would take up about 20 minutes so that's nearly half of my lunch time taken up. If the computer room was open I could hide in there for about half an hour until the next lesson. I'd worked out different ways to get through the break.

During one particular lesson, I was put in a group with people I didn't like so during break time I walked out. I wasn't bothered about the consequences; I just couldn't cope with being around people who I thought would be thinking horrible things about me.

My GCSE results weren't as good as they could have been but I was just so pleased when it had all ended.

That was pretty much my high school life summed up. I've spoken about everything that went on outside the classroom but haven't really spoken about what happened inside it so the next few sub-headings will cover that.

Guidance

In the early years of high school I had a personal tutor who sat in lessons with me. I didn't want to do this at first because I thought people would make fun of me having an adult sat with me when nobody else did. I needed the help but I did everything I could just to stop it because I wanted to fit in with everybody. In my 2nd year when I stopped seeing my personal tutor, it was advised I had a mentor. It took lots of persuading but my mum finally got me to agree to see him. Looking back it was great because lots of pupils don't have that option at school but I didn't think that way at the time. At first, I only agreed to see him if I didn't have to talk. I don't understand the logic looking back but that's the way it was. Very soon into my first session though I was chatting away to this guy I'd never spoken to before. Football was the breakthrough. If someone spoke about football to me, I would forget everything else and start waffling without any self conscience. The majority of the time I'd become a bit too intense and waffle on about details that not many would pick up on. I would remember the exact positions of the teams in the table that same week and who scored in what minute. I even got my mentor to set up a fantasy league team. I did it using my friends e-mail address and couldn't stop laughing when he complained to me he was getting random e-mails under someone else's name.

I came to really like my mentor. Not only did it help speaking to someone who actually listened to me but also it meant I got to skip certain lessons each week. I don't know how I'd have got through school without his help; he could make me see sense without making me feel silly. I remember once having a discussion about shoes. I used to wear shoes a size too small because people made fun of me having big feet, and because of that I have crooked toes to this day. He eventually talked me into wearing shoes that were the right size though the damage to my toes had already been done. If I was a bit quiet, he would tell me and after seeing him it made me feel more confident. We became friends outside of school too which I'll talk about later on.

Teachers

Teachers were always told about my diagnosis but I never really felt that they understood what it meant. It was a nightmare if my teacher was a woman and her hair would touch me when leaning over to help me with my work, I didn't want anyone's hair anywhere near me. I even felt like the teachers were against me in class, nothing to do with their hair touching me but because I didn't understand the content of what was being taught. I would be asked a question in front of the whole class and be laughed at because I didn't know. I'd be accused of not listening but that wasn't the case. I tried to make more effort to understand but I just couldn't. It didn't matter how easy it was, I just could not understand. If I were to understand something then it would have to be drilled into me at least 10 times.

I felt like a fool if I asked for help so I preferred to be told off even though I knew I wasn't doing anything wrong. I would get really upset over it.

That's pretty much all there is to say about teachers. It followed a very regular pattern and I was never one to communicate much with them.

Lessons

I did generally struggle in lessons. My pencil case had to be in a specific place on the desk, in a straight line and not an inch out. That wasn't the reason for my struggles though; it was just an added bonus.

Whenever a teacher wrote on the board and told the class to copy it, I would have to write it word for word or not at all. Even if the teacher had made a spelling mistake I would have to copy it. If a teacher turned to the next slide too quickly I would enter meltdown inside my head. There would be a blockage and I wouldn't copy anything else after that and get told off for doing no work. I couldn't understand things unless they were word for word.

Mainly in my earlier years, I couldn't understand what the teacher was saying if it was being said to a full table of students. It didn't matter how simple it was, I couldn't grasp it. A teacher would usually explain to me one to one after telling everyone else. Once I knew what was going on, I completed the work before everyone else in the class despite having less time. That's a good example of how my mind works. It can be very difficult to understand the most simple of things but when I do understand I can get the job done very quickly. How many times have I said that now? I told you I repeated myself. Anyway, it's very like writing this book for me. It can take me weeks just to plan it out but once I'm actually writing, it just flows out and I write pages in a time I didn't think was possible.

A lot of the concerns I had came from potential behaviour from other classmates, I remember once in Geography we had a day planned where everyone in the class would individually speak to a video camera and conduct a weather report. I deliberately made myself sick so I didn't have to go in and got extremely worked up about it. I sometimes even went to the extent of sticking 2 fingers down my throat and making myself gag. I did this sometimes in school so I could be sent home. There was another occasion in the same class where we were put in groups to make a volcano. I didn't read my friends body language and ended up making him cry because I didn't understand what to do. Our volcano won a prize but I didn't want to go in after falling out with my friend and didn't get the prize. I wasn't bothered. I didn't care about a stupid volcano made of newspaper; it had no relevance to me.

I was pretty good at Maths before I got a teacher I didn't like. After all, numbers were my guilty pleasure. I didn't like teachers who were very sure of themselves. Very cocky and suffering from little man syndrome (can I say that?). Let's be honest, it was true. A lot of the bullies fit a similar description. I'm not talking just about Maths, but any subject.

It's strange, the 2 lessons I really didn't like in school are subjects I take seriously now. Religious Education and Music. I'd grown an intense dislike for Music as soon as a secondary school teacher tried to get me to sing, I just mimed but I never forgot it so never took the lesson seriously after that. I felt that singing was a girl's thing and I knew I wasn't good at all; I was also very self conscious. My facial expressions didn't help either. I could have been singing a very up-tempo song but going by my face you'd think I was singing something at a funeral. I even mimed at church before I had any singing lessons; I still do if I'm not familiar with the hymn.

R.E. I didn't like at all. I went to a catholic high school so I didn't agree with some of it anyway and back then I wasn't a believer. I took things other students would say literally. A rather embarrassing example of this was during an R.E. Exam. The students had previously joked about what the Golden Rule was relating to. It was relating to the fact you should treat others as you would like to be treated but the students would joke about the rule being to protect your tool followed by a very quick punch to the nuts. I took that literally and I actually wrote that as an answer in the exam. Needless to say I got 0 marks for it.

English was difficult for me too. Stories had to be realistic and I couldn't write fiction. I could be creative in some ways but in my mind it had to be realistic. I could never write about zombies, ghosts and aliens. I also had to imagine myself in the role of the main character. It still applies to this day. Everything I write relates to real events that are actually going on.

Some may say my speech is pretty good but I never actually passed English at GCSE level. Some parts were very good but others I struggled with.

Trips

School trips were very much the same. I disliked them because it was out of my routine and I always feared sitting on my own on the coach. It was the same with swimming lessons in year 4.

On one occasion I had to dress up as a Tudor. What was the point? I just looked ridiculous and gained nothing from the experience other than being laughed at because I looked silly. There were a couple of trips though I have to say I quite enjoyed and they were both with my business class in secondary school, probably the only class where I felt totally comfortable. We went to the zoo once and I liked that because there were animals and we also visited an art museum which was interesting.

I didn't like museums generally though. Others were fascinated with neck chains with bullets on. Forgive me if I'm wrong but I thought bullets were meant to kill people, why would someone want to wear 1 on their neck? I don't really understand that.

Other students would look forward to mufti days when you didn't have to wear uniform, but not me. What if people didn't like my clothes? I didn't have the money to buy decent clothes and never started wearing jeans until after I'd left.

Later Study

I came out of High School with 7 GCSE's/equivalents in Graphics, Science and Business Studies. I didn't try at all and was a little disappointed that I just missed out on getting a C in Art, but I'd left the preparation till last minute. Like with all exams, it took me a while to get going. In one of my English papers I had 2 hours to complete it, I just sat there looking at the paper for an hour and by time I got into my stride the exam had ended. I would understand the questions better if someone verbally read them out to me but I didn't want to ask.

I liked the fact I didn't have to sit with everyone else in the main hall for exams, but I felt very nervous being called out in front of the whole year hearing little sniggers in the background as I was walking in. I sat in a classroom upstairs and was able to relax a lot more. This didn't help with my results though.

I was good at Maths and I.T. but failed both because I didn't get on with the teachers. I re-sat both of these straight away in college and passed them first time with flying colours. I still don't understand that flying colours phrase but I think it fits in well here.

I studied a Public Services National Diploma course for 2 years but didn't like the fact that half the class consisted of those who had bullied me at primary school. All had seemed to be forgotten but it was still very uncomfortable for me. It was after a suicide attempt in January 2008 that I had to be moved down a class because I'd fallen too far behind. My mind just wasn't in the right place and I was suffering badly with depression though I won't go into that here as we're talking about study.

My new class included mainly nice people but I still

didn't form any close friendships. I came out with a National Certificate and did the minimum I had to do to pass. Most weeks we went out on trips to do things like skiing, hiking and camping but it was out of my routine for me and I didn't like that. If I'd gone out of college hours I'd probably have enjoyed it a lot more.

After finishing at college I went to university and got my Foundation Degree in Business and Management. It took me 2 years. It couldn't be done locally so there was a lot of travelling involved but it was the name of the place that swayed me. It shared a name with a safari park and based on that I enrolled despite not knowing anything about the college. I still didn't form any real close friendships; I felt like an outsider and all the others lived locally.

I decided to stay on for a 3rd year to get my Honours Degree. I just wanted to get the qualification; I wasn't bothered about making friends or enjoying the experience. I didn't want to become involved in any of the nightlife; I just turned up to lectures and left straight afterwards. My mind still wasn't in the right place but I did what needed to be done. I didn't attend the graduation just like I didn't attend 'prom night' at high school. I didn't enjoy either experience so I didn't see why I should go. I didn't want to rewrite any of these memories; I would feel like I was lying to myself.

Very soon after finishing university I spent 6 weeks at a Personal Training Academy. I mainly kept myself to myself. Like with anywhere else I've studied, I've not kept in touch with anyone as I've not really formed any close friendships. I knew I found it hard socially so I just accepted it and got on with the work. Again, I did what I had to but I didn't go out of my way to enjoy the experience. I just wanted the qualification so I could progress onto the next step.

Now I'm more limited health wise, I have to feel I'm progressing all the time. I'm doing further studies in Theology and in Nutrition. I don't particularly enjoy it but I like knowing I'll have a qualification and it'll help me with future projects.

You can see that I wasn't good at making friends and gradually through each course I started to realise more and more that maybe I'm just not meant to be mixing because it made me feel so uncomfortable. I tried to alter my mindset and it worked.

Irlen Syndrome

Whilst at college I was diagnosed with Irlen Syndrome (I seem to be riddled with syndromes). I finally thought I'd found an answer to my problems despite knowing I still had Aspergers. It was like I tried my best to forget about having the condition and I wanted to find something else that could've explained all the problems I had. I didn't like knowing these problems were lifelong.

Irlen Syndrome causes eye problems for many people because it alters the way they see things. These eye problems are based on their visual perception. The eyes are not the main source of the problem. The problems are caused by the way in which the brain interprets the visual information that is being sent through the eyes. Having Irlen Syndrome prevents many people from reading effectively and efficiently. Individuals with Irlen Syndrome perceive reading material and/or their environment differently. They must constantly make adaptations or compensate for their eye problems. Individuals are often unaware of the extra energy and effort they are putting into reading and perception.

(Taken from www.irlen.org.uk)

You can see from the definition above why I thought this diagnosis could be an answer to my problems. It would have explained why I found it very difficult to read and interpret information. It could have explained why I found homework so hard and why my concentration span was almost non-existent. It was more hope than actual thinking.

I did however find it easier to read using coloured tints but the problems were still the same and I was disappointed. To this day I wonder what it must be like to be able to understand things easily.

I became a little self conscious about wearing rose tinted specs but I knew there was a saying I could make a joke of so came to quite like them. The glasses and coloured tint still help me now and whilst it aids with reading, it's had no effect on how I take in information.

Missed Opportunities

I look back at times I have studied in a classroom and do wish certain things could have been different. I wish I could have found it easier making friends and been able to keep in touch and form good relationships. I wish I'd tried harder with my work rather than just doing the minimum amount required. But I don't like having regrets and I'm glad I got through the study I did whilst suffering with bad depression. Depression I feel that was largely caused by having this condition.

Since having my last book published in 2014 I have really started to feel that I can be myself and not worry about others opinions. It's as if everything that has previously happened has been put behind me and has prepared me for now. I feel my life can really start now.

Chapter 4: Work Worries

In work, I need to know exactly what I'm doing. I can get lots done if it's clear in my mind. If something isn't very clear then I will really struggle. You'll see a pattern forming as you read on, hopefully.

I wanted to be a policeman or a prison guard after leaving school. I veered more towards being a prison officer because I liked the idea of routine. Set times for everything, smart uniform and doing good for the community all sounded very appealing to me. The only thing that stopped me was my diagnosis. I knew my mind wasn't programmed efficiently enough in certain areas to be able to cope with the constant pressure.

My first taste of work came as a paper boy. I liked the idea of making money from a young age counting every bit of change I had. I would even pick coppers up off the floor and put them in my change jar. I didn't understand why people would throw 1p coins onto the floor because all money adds up. Back in the day it could have paid for a cola bottle from the corner shop. I always had the idea that every single penny helped towards something. I worked at 3 different paper shops, only changing when I moved house which was quite frequent in those days. I would often work 7 days a week and at 1 point had an afternoon round as well as a morning one. I liked it because I got to deliver to all the posh houses and I thought 1 day I would make it a priority to live in a house like that. I always felt that I would make money but never really knew how. I remember getting a 30p bonus for working on a bank holiday on top of my weekly wage of just over £10 and that was only 10 years ago. My bonus wouldn't even have paid for a mars bar. There was a game on the Gameboy called 'Paperboy': I was like the guy in that, trying to deliver papers in a record time. However, I didn't like it when my round was changed with someone else's because it always took me a while to get used to my own. It was a change of routine and I really struggled with that. It always made me feel as though I couldn't cope and I wanted to leave. My sense of direction was terrible so I took a copy of the round back to my mum: she would find the different addresses on the map and then write me out a map of my own. She used to tell me I had to rotate the piece of paper if I turned down certain streets but I couldn't do that. I always used to end up ringing her on my mobile phone mid round. She got used to it and would leave her phone under her pillow expecting a call at around 7:20am every morning. "I'm lost again" I would say: she would get the map book out which was also always under her pillow. I used to like the Saturday round because it meant I got home before anyone else in the house was up. This meant I could use the computer (had to share back in those days) and look up previous wrestling events and type in more football data. This would be a good start to the weekend for me because it would settle my mind. It meant my mind was a little more free when I met friends for bike rides or games of football.

Experience

I did my high school work experience in 2006 which was for a period of 2 weeks. It was split between 2 different places. I worked 1 week in a gym and the 2nd week I was working with animals which was perfect for me. Working at the gym was great. I really enjoyed that because it was in a gym, an environment I was comfortable in by that point. I also got to wear my own clothes which made me feel more at ease. I liked it because there was very little interaction with people. I don't think they knew what to do with me to be honest. 1 afternoon I had to try and repair a rubber dinghy (a duck or a dragon I think) and go out to a local shop to buy the right things. I didn't know what I was doing but I gave it a go. I was located above the swimming pools and it felt very secretive. I liked the fact no one knew where I was. I felt a bit like Batman: I'd never seen that but I had an idea of what he'd get up to... maybe not repairing dinghies though. There was netting and it felt a little in the rafters. Despite hours of trying to repair the dinghy I failed, despite my best efforts. The thing was I don't think the staff were that bothered as the dinghy hadn't been used for a few years. It was also during the 2006 world cup so I spent a lot of my time watching the matches whilst cleaning the equipment or 'resting' on the bike. A lot of people hate cleaning but I thought it was ok because I knew exactly what needed to be done. I was ok if I knew exactly what needed cleaning, in what place and at what time: that suited me. The rest of the time I just played on my phone trying to browse the internet (the middle button wouldn't work as the phone was previously in a carrier bag, which got stuck in my bike wheel and went flying in bits across a graveyard whilst pedalling). The staff at the gym were generally very nice but I always felt awkward and tried to avoid any sort of interaction. I would deliberately clean equipment in the quietest areas of the gym.

The 2nd week I spent working with animals but surprisingly I didn't enjoy it as much. Not because of the animals but because of the other people there. I loved the animals; I grew an attachment to a big dog called Dusty who would greet me each morning. I would sit in his kennel and talk to him for a while and despite not hearing words, I had better conversations with that dog than anyone else in the building. I was left on my own to do things but I didn't like that. I needed reminding on how to do certain things because I didn't understand as easily as others but they didn't seem to realise that, despite being told I had Aspergers. 1 afternoon I was just left to mop the floor of a big room for an hour. I tried my hardest but it wasn't good enough. I didn't know where to find anyone and ended up being given 'simpler' tasks like taking the dogs for a walk around the back. This suited me much better. A ferret there had just had an operation and I was told to take it for a walk. It kept flopping over and didn't want to walk but it was fun. My best friend at school was working there too so when I was left on my own and couldn't find anyone, I would see what he was doing. As a result I was sent home early 1 day and told not to go back in because they didn't need me. No-one seemed to really be in charge and I needed someone to supervise me closely but this never happened. The lack of supervision there was very difficult for me to cope with.

I had a couple more work placements a few years later which were during my time at university. For my 1st year placement, my official title was 'Marketing Assistant': I sealed envelopes with invitations in them in record time but other than that I didn't actually do anything. I had to attend a conference 1 day at Wigan's DW stadium. I spent the day there with my tutor but even afterwards I didn't have a clue what I was doing there really. I just liked wearing my suit and being at a football ground. It turned out only a couple of people turned up despite sending dozens of invitations. I left it too late as usual. I just remember being embarrassed that day as I underestimated the cost of the train fare. I had to ask my tutor for the train fare home. I found it quite difficult talking to my tutor and, like at school,

I never liked to ask for help as I felt silly. As shown here, it meant the job I was given wasn't done efficiently and neither party had benefitted.

For my 2nd placement whilst at university I worked in a financial advisors office. I actually really enjoyed this. It was formal; I liked wearing a suit because it looked smart. Most of the time I knew exactly what I was doing and I was helping the company to save money on certain things which spurred me on to do the best I could. My supervisor was great and was also a good friend of mine. He helped me throughout my time there and assisted me with calculations. I'd potentially saved the company £22,194.77 per year which made me happy. I felt a sense of accomplishment. It made me want to continue in this line of work. The office environment suited me: cups of tea at certain times and a lunch break at a particular time too. A very specific goal to reach meant I was in my comfort zone. That was the difference: if things were fully explained to me then I knew I was capable of doing a good job. Managers and supervisors made all the difference to me. I also liked the social interaction there which, as I explain in my next chapter, is usually a big problem for me. Everyone else in the office bar the manager and supervisor were all female: that made me feel more comfortable. I preferred talking to females rather than males: I can often feel a little intimidated around men due to the stuff that went on in school. That's just me: I'd rather talk about fashion or who was voted off X-factor the night before than talk about how much I'd had to drink or how many ladies I'd kissed at the weekend.

Not only that but I enjoyed finding figures from the computer and I liked seeing them all together in a list. I worked very hard while I was there and got top marks for the presentation.

The main point of the project was to find out the ROI (Return on Investment) whilst I was there. I worked on 4 different areas within the company: e-mails, investments and pensions, stationery and local awareness. The return on investment turned out to be 1337% and as I mentioned earlier, I potentially saved the company £22,194.77. This was very specific and I felt it was a job well done.

Customer Service

Other than delivering my papers, my next 2 jobs

were in fast food restaurants. I tolerated the 1st 1 but hated the 2nd job. The 1st job was at a holiday camp and so the contract was for the season and I didn't renew it at the end. The trip to the interview should have been an early sign. My friend gave me a lift and he turned out to be my supervisor. He had to change his tyre on the way so we were late. He hadn't noticed that a pair of scissors were stuck in his tyre. I got on with everyone but I didn't like the way things were run. Some of the staff would smoke drugs during the break and to be honest I did on 1 occasion as I was sick of the job. It made flipping the burgers a little more exciting for the rest of that day I have to say. There would often be late finishes which meant drunk people would inevitably turn up. Certain events would be held for different groups of people. Swingers night was my least favourite. A sleazy night with greasy chips wasn't good. My dogs loved the leftover popcorn chicken I took home for them which was at least something salvaged from the experience. I hated serving customers but I couldn't very well avoid it. It didn't help that I had a big quiff and peroxide blonde hair whilst people were continually asking if I was the 3rd member of Jedward. I didn't like that because I looked nothing like them. On my last shift I actually lost it a little with my supervisor because I didn't think it was fair that I'd been put on the till more than him. It was very out of character for me but I felt pushed to the limit. I found it hard being face to face with customers. I bellowed "Don't speak to me like that" and we didn't talk for the whole shift afterwards. It was 9pm-9am and I was at college at the time so it was tough going. It didn't help that my supervisor was a classmate from college and gave me a lift home. I got on with him in college. Height had nothing to do with it however I didn't like being told what to do by someone not only my own age but someone I could barely see over the counter. I didn't know where he was half the time.

Work at the 2nd fast food place was horrible... it made working at the other place seem luxurious. The manager was the worst I'd ever had the displeasure of working under. I only lasted 3 weeks because I couldn't put up with her any longer. I was wiping the tables and all of a sudden she stormed towards me, snatched the paper towels from me and stormed off leaving me to look like a lemon because I couldn't carry on with the cleaning. I tried to hide round the back as much as possible and preferred washing up; I'd do anything to do the washing up. It meant I didn't have to face customers and I could be left to work on my own. I could work quickly doing something like that but working on the tills was very difficult for me. The manager was so horrible and yet she had her tongue down another member of staffs throat round the back whilst I was trying to grasp the work. The word hypocrite came to mind. I really struggled and no-one really helped me. I felt it was pointless mentioning my Aspergers diagnosis as I didn't want to be labelled by it and I didn't want to appear like I was making excuses. It was very hard as it was pressurised and things were changing all the time. My mind couldn't process everything quickly enough.

My longest job lasted just over 2 years. I worked at a pub and it was really out of my comfort zone initially. At times it was very fast paced and you always had to be on the ball. I got used to it once I knew what glasses went where but I struggled when things were moved and when I had to remember long orders. It took me a while to adjust when there were changes in the routines. There was constant interaction with customers and I found it very hard, especially as I sometimes felt intimated by male customers who were drinking. It was an environment

I would never have mixed in if I hadn't worked there. The staff were great and they probably figured out I was a little different: they accepted me though and I always felt included as a part of the group. That was the difference. When I was working around understanding people I could work a lot more efficiently. I might have been slightly different to the majority of people but I got the job done. The manager was strict but fair: if you did what you were employed to do then she was very pleasant and that was fair enough. I liked that. It was quite black and white and I like it when things are like that. I know exactly where I stand.

I managed to incorporate my obsession for numbers into my work routine. Complimentary sausages would be put out on the bar on a Friday and Saturday night. When I helped myself to some I had to have the slices in sets of 3's. If I had 3 and felt like another 1, I would have to take another 2 and round it to 5. Then the lucky 7. Then I'd round it up to 10. I would never go over that amount as the sausages were supposed to be for the customers. If I ever got anywhere near that amount then you knew it was a quiet night. There were chip barms on a Monday night and they were bigger so I liked having them in sets of 2. I knew having 3 was a bit cheeky so I limited it to 2 but I wasn't happy with just 1. I wanted a pair.

The only reason I had to leave the pub was to due to my increasing health problems and was nothing to do with Aspergers.

Confrontation

After I'd graduated from university, I was offered a job within days that sounded a little too good to be true but I decided to go along with it. The 1st day actually went ok, the other people there were great and there weren't really any issues socially which was unusual for me, though by this point I'd learned a lot about socialising. I started to get the impression that the whole thing was corrupt though. We were all told in a presentation to not mention certain things to customers when trying to sell our product. My supervisor also gave me the worst advice ever. "Always throw all of your eggs into one basket". If I'd done that then I would have ended up with no job at all. Mind you, I couldn't take him that seriously after he'd told me that he would easily win The Apprentice if he ever applied. I asked him why he didn't and he said he was too good for it.

Potentially it was a very highly paid job but it was extremely results driven. If you didn't reach your targets then you were out. I didn't like that. The days were very long and the typical daily shift would be close to 12 hours. I had to randomly approach people who were quite prepared to verbally attack me as I was trying to sell them a product that I didn't even believe in myself. It was the worst possible job you could ever have picked for me. I wasn't very thick skinned at that point so any negative comment would finish me off. Every time I arrived home in the evening I was too tired to even have food. I could barely move by the end of the day as it was so tiring.

I realised pretty quickly that it just wasn't for me and I didn't even care about the potential income. The night before I'd decided to leave. I couldn't sleep, sick with worry. I was dreading having to tell my manager I wasn't going to continue. He was absolutely fine and shook my hand but that moment caused me severe stress leading up to it. I worked myself up so much. I was as white as a ghost and felt physically sick. This is what it was like when I worked myself up so much. I knew it was coming but

I couldn't stop it. I couldn't handle it... but everything was soon ok after that.

I'm going to add my time spent working at a gym here too as there was a fair bit of confrontation involved in that too. I'd just qualified as a Personal Trainer and although I knew and enjoyed what I was doing, I had difficulties when dealing with people face to face. I didn't like approaching people. I knew how I'd feel if I was approached whilst I was working out. I felt I was invading their space and it was very difficult. I put myself in their situation and knew I wouldn't want to be approached by me. It was the wrong job at the wrong time as I was going through several doctors' appointments and had referrals to wait on. There was no routine because it was up to me what hours I worked and I had to fit in with what the other Personal Trainers were doing. Even the small classes I held weren't always at the same times due to the fact that other things were going on. It was a very small gym and a bit overcrowded.

The classes gave me a little confidence and experience but in just a few weeks I had to leave and cut my losses as my health started to decline and it was only 2 months after this that I was diagnosed with ME/CFS. It was very disappointing as I had invested a lot of both time and money into this venture.

Other Work

In the midst of my previous work experiences I worked part-time as a painter and decorator before I started my Foundation Degree. I got used to it but it wasn't natural to me at all. I felt a bit of a fool sometimes and at times I felt like I was being patronised. I didn't like doing new things and liked sticking to what I knew. I wasn't used to it at all and remember after my first day saying "Are you sure?" when given my wages. I was used to helping out voluntarily and thought it would be rude to assume I'd be paid despite being taken on to do a job. If things weren't said to me word for word then I'd always be unsure. I didn't like getting my hands dirty and felt the need to wash them every few minutes and couldn't take my mind away from it if they hadn't been washed. I liked it when I was left alone to complete tasks.

I've also helped out other people with this sort of work and, like with other jobs, a lot depended on who I was working with. If they were understanding and treated me like everyone else then I proved I actually could work efficiently.

I recall a rather embarrassing occasion when I was helping out decorating round the back of our church. I lacked common sense and the paint tray wasn't very secure. The whole lot managed to find its way onto my head... when my hair was bleached peroxide blonde. This meant that half my head was bright red and the other half was bright white. I quickly cycled home to get in the shower but I was stopped half way home. A journalist for the local newspaper waved over to me and mistook me for someone else. I can only assume that he was looking for someone who had a very bloody face that had just been beaten up. As I arrived home, I got into the shower and again lacked common sense. Can I say that's because my mind works differently or do I just not have any common sense? Anyway, I used bleach to get the solid mass of paint from my head and forgot to close my eyes. It was pretty painful but I learned from it. I've never done that again since then.

Interviews

I'm going to dedicate the last sub-heading of this chapter to interviews. I've mentioned all previous work experience but I've not mentioned my behaviour in interviews. Not that it's anything erratic, but this sub-heading means there's 5 in this chapter and you know I'm a fan of that number.

Generally speaking, I would be happy if every shift at work was an interview. Some people find interviews pretty daunting but I quite enjoy them. People ask me questions that I've prepared for; it's not really any different to any other social interaction I have. Preparation is needed for that but from this particular situation, I might get a job out of it. For me, there were always vast similarities between interviews, psychiatrists and friends. They all followed the same format.

"Hi, how are you?"
"Fine thanks, you?"
"Good, so Barry..."

Then a bit of waffle would proceed and it would be

very formal.

My biggest problem was shaking hands with the interviewer, and eye contact of course. That was worse but I'll explain all of that in the next chapter.

I wasn't too bad if it was a formal situation so it didn't bother me too much. I always made a point at the end to mention my Asperger's diagnosis. I didn't want to bring it up straight away as I didn't want to be pre-judged or labelled by it. It seemed to work.

I once applied for a job at a funeral directors. I remember those around me being confused as to why I had applied for the position but it made perfect sense to me. When it comes to work, I've always found working in quiet office like environments suit me. I find that I get easily distracted in noisy surroundings and I get much more done working in a quieter, formal place. The job was very specific and it wasn't exactly going to be a very jolly place was it? I had trouble laughing so I had the perfect excuse not to if I landed that job. Routine suited me and the job wouldn't have phased me at all. They were impressed with the interview but I could only work 2 days a week due to study and they wanted somebody who could work more hours. They were impressed that I seemed to know a fair bit about spreadsheets on the computer, well in a way it was my niche. I just probably didn't use them for the most productive things.

There was 1 interview that went horribly wrong but it didn't bother me as I wasn't too sure what the job was anyway when I applied. Something to do with care work. It wouldn't have suited me to be honest due to the physical contact with clients which would be unavoidable.

I would tell you more about interviews but without sounding big headed, I got the job for all the others I attended. If I'm being honest, I am probably better at giving an interview than actually dealing with the jobs I have had. I can work out the right things to say whilst remaining as honest as possible.

Chapter 5: Social Inconvenience

This was probably my most enjoyable chapter to write as it describes a lot of my traits very well. People who know me will now see the reasons for how I am and that in itself feels like a massive weight has been taken from my shoulders. I don't want people to feel sorry for me or to treat me differently just because I might do things in a different way. After all, this makes perfect logical sense to me.

Talking

1 of the 1st things you probably think of when hearing the word social is talking.

It's a funny thing isn't it? Sometimes you can't stop me but other times you can't get a word out of me. I like to think of myself as observant. I choose when to speak. I pick the right moments, although my timing could be a little better. A lot of what I say has been pre-planned. There's a list inside my head of things I'd like to say when talking to a particular person and I'll try to pick the right moments to bring them into the conversation. Why? Well, from being a child, looking back I would get too carried away if someone spoke to me, and I'd take it to the next level and maybe 'freak' someone out. What I mean by this is that I would sometimes recite certain subjects that no-one would usually pick up on. Things that usually had little relevance, but which showed I was a little 'too involved in the subject'. It would knock my confidence because an insult of some sort would then come my way. I was trying to be friendly but people were making fun of me. It made me very quiet throughout school which I explained in the last chapter and a lot of that was because of the fear that someone might say something nasty or I may say the wrong thing because I knew it was a weakness of mine.

I've picked up little bits over the years about what others like to talk about whilst I totally disregarded what I wanted to talk about. Of course there's the usual "Hi, how are you?", "What you been up to?" (The typical MSN hotmail talk growing up, speaking to people you knew but were too scared to speak to in person... or was that just me?).

"What have you been up to?" That's the question... I will pick up on every detail you give me from the answer to that, that way it gives me a good foundation on where to take the conversation. For example, I'm not a fan on nightlife and disagree with a lot of what it represents, but that doesn't mean I'm not willing to listen to someone else talk about it. Others will talk because they want to; I talk because it's a personal achievement and sometimes a necessity.

If someone then asks me what I've been up to, despite being active on social media, I'm a very private person. I have developed a knack of quickly turning the conversation back to that person. I avoid talking about myself. Sure, I can talk about things I like but then I know I might get a little carried away and talk very technically about a subject. In my head I filter each of my subjects and choose only certain people I talk about them. I can talk about football but as soon as I start to refer to league positions or previous results, then I know I've lost them unless they're an avid fan like me. I can talk about writing a book but as soon as I mention what it's about (like M.E.) then I've sometimes picked up different signs which have indicated to me that someone is not interested. I will remember that and never bring up that topic again unless I make a social blunder. My conversations tend to be all about the other person because I feel I have nothing worthwhile to add to anything else that will interest anyone. There are the odd exceptions but they don't come around too often.

Having said that, I don't often have a clue as to what someone is talking about so I'll go along with it. I feel silly if I ask them what certain words mean. I will use some words which I know fit well with what I'm saying but I won't actually know what they mean if someone asks me. A good old 'google' searching session for definitions of words will takes place after this has happened. One definition isn't enough though, I have to get at least 3 definitions to make sure I have the right meaning because I know I can understand things differently to others.

I can also come across as very intense when talking, but I don't always realise this. I've developed a dry sense of humour to fit in with this. People don't know if I'm being serious or not and that's part of the humour. It gives me that get out of jail card if I say something inappropriate. I can have the odd social blunder and I use this to try to cover it up. One thing I really dislike is speaking on the telephone. I don't often answer the phone first time. I like to see who it is trying to get in touch and then think about what they might be ringing me for. I will then think of a few different scenarios and how to approach them. That way, I come across as a lot chattier than I used to, because I've worked out how I operate socially.

If I'm put on the spot then my mind goes. Even if I know something, I will forget because I can't cope with the pressure of having to give a quick answer. My mind doesn't work that quickly.

Another reason I don't like telephone conversations is because I can't see the person. I can't attempt to read their body language, and their expression could be different to how they sound. I find it hard understanding the tone of voice. They could have me on loudspeaker laughing... but maybe that's just my paranoia...

On a positive note, no one over a phone line can actually touch me or see my lack of expression. Another positive is that at least if I spill my drink of water (never far away from me) then the phone will cut off and I don't have to talk (a little joke about my co-ordination which you'll read about later on).

If I raise my voice half an octave or so during a conversation then my tone of speech might come across as interesting rather than being monotone. It's good for singing practice, multitasking in a way. Keeping in tune.

I used to like communicating through text messages on my mobile phone because it gave me time to think about my replies and to add the necessary symbols required such as an exclamation mark or a kiss. My general rule is 1 kiss for a lady, 2 if they're a good friend and 3 or more if I fancy them. I always used to be very quick at replying to messages, no matter how busy I was. But then I learned to understand that others have busy lives and they don't see replying as a priority, and it made me think that I need to take the same approach. I've lost a few acquaintances due to this but then who wants conversations that are one sided? If someone doesn't reply to me then I won't follow it up. People that genuinely have an interest in you will stick around and vice-versa.

Touching

I'm now going to move onto the areas I've struggled with most when it comes to body language.

I didn't used to understand body language at all. If I was too close to someone, I didn't know where to look because eye contact was intimidating. If someone jokingly told me to shut up I would take it literally and say nothing for the rest of the day. They'd ask what was up but I'd say I was ok. Even if they said things were ok, I still found it awkward afterwards. I also had a thing about body posture; I would stand up so straight it sometimes hurt my spine. There are so many random facts I could focus on but I'll take you through the main points starting with 'Touching'.

First and foremost, I don't like being touched. Where has the hand that's touched me been? If you've got a bit of dirt under your finger nail then it's not very nice if it's heading my way. Has that person been picking their nose? Not washing their hands after going to the toilet? Have they been touching other people who are dirty? I've learned over the years to tolerate it. After all, if one day I'm going to get married then I'm going to have to tolerate being touched aren't I? I can't expect everyone to give their hands a good wash with soap before they touch me so I'll tend to make it as awkward as possible if someone goes to touch me.

If I want to say hello to someone I'll shout over, not touch them. Again, where have their hands been? I don't know, what if they'd just been to the toilet and then touched me straight after? I'd have to put my clothes in the wash then. At least if a bird pooped on me I'd know where it came from. If someone touched my face and a flannel wasn't on standby, what a nightmare that would be. If someone kissed me... even worse. Someone else's saliva on my skin, disgusting. What if they touched the last person they were with and they didn't smell very nice? I'd prefer it if someone kept their hands to themselves unless they asked for my permission. Keep your hands to yourself please.

If my mum hugged me or a friend touched my shoulder it made me feel very uncomfortable. Why would they want to touch me? What are they gaining from it? My shoulder feels strange because someone else has touched it. If I wanted someone to touch my shoulder I'd have done it myself. I couldn't understand how girls touched me. Surely that meant they fancied me. I would only ever touch a girl I fancied. I'm talking about actually touching, maybe a hand or shoulder.

I'll tolerate it if I fancy them or have a very close connection but that doesn't always apply. If they're wearing a fluffy animal print coat then it might sway me. I'm probably closer to my mum than anyone else but there's an unwritten agreement that no hugs or kisses are allowed. She might grab my arm to make it look like we're touching in a photograph but that's pushing it a little. She pushed her luck one time at Christmas and luckily I was in a good mood, there was still a little friction for a few hours though.

Basically, if I've ever touched you then you should feel honoured. If it's happened a number of times then re-read the last paragraph and work out where you fit in. I'm black and white like that. If you don't fit in then I have a lot of explaining to do.

I'm very uncomfortable around flirty people for this reason so it's strange that a fair few girls I've been out with did happen to be very flirty. Maybe opposites attract? They probably saw me as a challenge but the reality was I was actually being serious. If I say something I mean it. I'm not playing hard to get. I'm just a bit strange, that's all. I don't mind them being flirty towards me if 1) no-one else is around and 2) they're not being flirty with everyone else. I don't want to be just another on a list. Allowing someone to be flirty with me is a pretty big deal in my eyes even if it's casual to someone else.

There was 1 time at a youth group when we all played a game and a very pretty girl went to sit on my knee but I wouldn't let her so she got upset. I felt terrible but I just didn't want anyone sitting on my knee. I feel embarrassed now looking back but my mind couldn't cope with physical contact in any way shape or form.

Maybe that's why I take the phrase "treat the body like a temple" literally. Would people touch a temple? It's why I'm very determined about health and keeping in shape. My motto if you like.

I don't really like shaking hands as you've probably gathered. I used to greet people on the door at church as I wanted to be involved but after shaking everyone's hand I would always jet off to the toilet to wash my hands. I couldn't settle otherwise. If I wanted to scratch my nose then I would use the side of my hand if I hadn't been able to wash them. Too many hands.

It made interviews awkward too, as I explained in the last chapter. I made a point of shaking hands and then craftily as I sat down I might rub my hand on the chair or my trouser leg. Pretend I had an itch or something. I just didn't like physical contact with others full stop.

Having said all this, I'm nowhere near as bad now. I've gradually learned to tolerate being hugged. It involves a lot of touching, it's a big deal for me and I'd have to feel incredibly close to the person I was hugging unless I had no choice in the matter i.e. if I was pounced on without warning.

I'm going to end this section with talking about saying goodbyes as I feel that would be appropriate for obvious reasons.

It's always awkward saying goodbye to a friend.

We've already established that I don't like hugging so they have to initiate it. There's usually a pause when we part ways. I think "Right, a hugs coming, brace yourself". If they're hugging other people then I don't want to be hugged too. It's a pretty big thing for me. To this day I don't hug my mum. She knows I don't like it so doesn't ask unless it's Christmas day; it doesn't cause as much friction as it did years ago though. My friends always hugged so it was good practice for me. I was always more comfortable hugging men. I was uncomfortable around women but with men it was different. Probably because I never had any female friends throughout my time at school and I never viewed females as friends, I was too shy around them. Also, I would've got a sore back because the majority of people I knew were smaller than me. A kiss on the cheek is a little awkward too as I have to work out a way to get past the hair in a split second. I like the look of lipstick but I'd find it really hard to kiss. What's in lipstick? The chemicals entering my mouth. I've just had a healthy tea; I don't want it mixed with chemicals.

Expression

Lack of expression has always been a problem of

mine and as stated before I amended my sense of humour to be dry. That way it would fit in with my rigid eyebrows. People don't know whether to laugh or take me seriously now. I play up to it... sometimes. It can often be interpreted in whichever way you want it to. It suits me because it continues to help me learn what is acceptable socially.

A few years back, people would make fun of me and it really got to me because I couldn't help the fact I didn't give much away. It wasn't just acquaintances either, it was teachers. One said I "looked like I wanted to kill someone". I thought to myself, "Just you wait till the lessons over". On a serious note, I didn't appreciate it so was always 'cold' with that teacher afterwards. It's not nice either when your 'friends' start laughing too. These days I can laugh it off and make a joke of it but back then I was like a snail that wanted to hide in its shell all the time but the shell had been stamped on and broken.

I'll give you an example of how expressionless I can appear. When I try to raise my eyebrows it physically hurts. I never raise my eyebrows even when I laugh. You will notice that the top half of my head always stays the same. My eyebrows only comfortably move sideways, achieved by tensing muscles in the back of my head. This is quite hard work so I find it easier not to show much expression at all. I've never shown any expression on my forehead. I had an obsession about getting a wrinkly forehead when I was younger.

A few years back when out on a date they picked up on this and made a little joke. Not exactly a great chat up line is it? At least my forehead won't need ironing out in 20 years time unless I have a major mid-life crisis.

Let's look at the positives here. It means I don't have to get surgery when I'm older.

You could tell me that someone had just died and I'd look exactly the same as if you'd just told me I'd won the lottery. Sometimes I was too afraid to show off any expression in case it wasn't appropriate or if people would laugh in case I came across a little too camp. My inside feelings were never portrayed by my outside expressions. They didn't work together so over the years I've had to study other's expressions as they've never come naturally to me. I had to be careful I didn't stare of course but it got me to the point where now I don't have to worry about my face. After all I can always make a joke of it.

Eye Contact

I can't have a conversation and keep eye contact, it's nigh on impossible. I'll often look away and give them a quick glance just to show I'm still interested but even that's a bit awkward. I can look quite shifty at times but I can't help that. You'll notice in a conversation with me that I will always initially look at you and then look away straight after. I try to focus on certain areas of the room I'm in so I have somewhere to look at. I can easily look at someone if they're not looking at me but when both sets of eyes meet I can't maintain contact, there's a trigger in my brain that makes me look away without even thinking. My heart will start racing if I hold eye contact for longer than what I deem is necessary. Someone looking me in the eye would feel like a gun shot. It's almost as if I could hear the bang as I quickly look away. When the 2 eyes meet, the trigger has gone.

A lot can depend on the person I'm in conversation with though. I'm generally ok with family as I've been brought up with them. Acquaintances are mainly awkward and partners can be Ok if the feelings are mutual.

Coordination

When I was younger and we moved house (which we did a lot of), I just couldn't grasp how to walk around block.

It was a very simple left out of house then left again left again, but what I couldn't get is the fact that it took me back home. Once I was any distance away from the house I would think I was lost so took a right turn.

I mentioned this previously as I spoke about my troubles with paper rounds too. I don't have these problems to this extent now but they are still there. My sense of direction is still pretty woeful and I even struggle to travel around my local area if I'm going somewhere I don't normally go. I have certain set routes. If I go out of town, after 10 times of showing me the way, there is still no guarantee that I will be able to follow the directions.

With regards to coordination, there is another thing that I struggle with on a day to day basis and that is spilling my constant drinks of water. It's a nightmare. I always drink water; fortunately it doesn't stain. This is a big advantage. If I drank blackcurrant or fizzy pop then all the carpets would have to be replaced on a regular basis.

It's like I can't quite work out how far the cup is to my mouth. A bit like missing when men aim for the toilet... although I don't do that of course. I'm very clean I'll have you all know.

I have always been prone to clumsiness. I was 1 of those who could trip over his own shoes at school. I'm not as bad now and I certainly don't trip over my own feet but I do have a tendency to bang into tables; it's also another way of spilling water unintentionally. I'll stub my toes on corners of furniture too; in fact maybe the reason my toes are so crooked isn't because I used to wear shoes too small but because they keep clashing with large items of furniture. Just a thought.

Social Events

Now you know about a few more of my characteristics when it comes to communicating, let's see how I cope in social situations. I found it hard in a way differentiating between talking and socialising at events but I felt they deserved a sub section each.

In a nut shell, people don't understand my humour and I don't understand theirs hence regular miscommunication. There's always the odd exception as with most things, but that person would either have to be as nutty as a fruit cake... or me.

Socialising is such a chore isn't it? The amount of preparation needed sometimes makes it seem not worthwhile. That's when social media comes in handy. I can take my time and actually give a decent, well thought out reply.

I've already briefly spoken about conversations but I'll go into a little more detail here. You could probably read my conversations from an autocue.

I'll dwell all through the night before if an event is coming up, especially if I don't really know the people well. I had an outing a few months back and couldn't think of anything else for 2 weeks before. It ruined those 2 weeks for me. I wasn't in control: I didn't know who was going to be there and didn't know how much I'd see of the people I knew quite well. I will spend a while the evening before thinking of possible questions I might be asked and how I would answer them. It's not only the night before though, it's as soon as I know about the event, so these thoughts could last for weeks. Others can put it out of their head for a while but I can't. I don't let on that I can't, but that's the truth. It's very difficult at times.

Even now, I can feel like I'm being undermined when talking about Aspergers. In the way that I'm a nice guy but not as good as others. I don't actually feel that myself but I feel that others can think that. I was out recently for a meal with a group. Someone just randomly told everyone I had Aspergers. I didn't like it because I only like to tell people when I'm ready for them to know. I like to have preset responses to possible questions. For example, if I'm invited out to a get together with a group, I like to know exactly how many are going and who they are.

I set myself specific aims for events like planned meals. I'll decide in advance that I'm going to crack a joke and if I achieve that then my goal has been reached and I can relax. If I'm on a roll then maybe I'll push my luck and crack another 1 if I feel the atmosphere is right. Telling someone they have nice hair or a nice top is always a bonus if I'm feeling rather spontaneous. However, I can't lie, so if I don't actually think anyone has really nice hair then it becomes a problem.

Anyway, here are the unwritten rules (well they are written actually if you're reading them but I would hope you know what I mean)... I don't actually make a list but these are the things that go through my head:-

1. If you invite me then make sure I know everyone who is going.

2. Do not change the time because I will have altered and adapted my routine to fit in with this.

3. Don't sit me next to someone I don't know because that's double the pressure for me to

deal with.

4. Don't ask me why I'm not drinking or why I haven't got a girlfriend.

5. Do try and sit next to me if I don't know anyone else.

Actually, after reading that, I wouldn't be surprised if I never got invited out again. I'm hard work aren't I? I don't insist these things have to be done but if any of these rules are broken then it upsets me and ruins the night because it unsettles me.

I always used to trust other people's judgements better than mine, especially in conversation. If they did something I knew was wrong I would still go along with it because I thought they knew better than me. I knew that my mind worked differently so always tried to take things from what other people said. I would never conflict or confront.

I would sometimes say something completely out of order when I was just trying to make conversation. Maybe make a joke about something inappropriate. It would destroy the confidence I had plucked up in the 1st place to tell the joke. I was back to square one. I might give away too much detail, someone may say "too much information", but I wouldn't understand why.

People could hint to me all day long and I still wouldn't pick up on it and I'd feel silly as a result.

1 to 1 is so much better for me. Errors can be pointed out more easily and I also feel more relaxed. I only have to prepare conversation for that 1 person; all of my attention is focused on them. There are certain things I'd be a little awkward with such as if someone were to ask me round for a 1 to 1 meal at their house. I wouldn't be comfortable with this. It would be too intimate for me to cope easily with.

I generally don't like going round to others houses either, and vice versa. My house is where I have my 'me time' and someone would have to be pretty special to be accepted into my little world. I'm very privative in that way. I would always prefer to meet someone in a public setting.

Going to concerts with friends is very awkward too, but it's not happened too often. I always feel uncomfortable when I'm asked because I don't like being a constant let down. I don't want to wave my arms up in the air or bang my head and get a sore neck. I'd rather just sit in my seat expressionless and (in my own mind) enjoy the concert. I don't care if it looks like I'm attending a funeral. I would still enjoy it just as much as everybody else there.

Honestly, I don't give a monkey's when I say this (it's a phrase I don't understand) but I'd much rather get involved with girly talk than lad talk. I mentioned this before and it's strange because I never spoke to any females at school but now I very rarely speak to males. In my experience, I've always found that females are more understanding of health conditions and the more deeper stuff in general which immediately puts me more at ease. Men would be a lot more likely to question why I didn't behave in a more 'fun' manner. Some would say, "You're good looking, why don't you do that?" when referring to general 'lad' behaviour. "Maybe because I have morals?"

There's also the fear of others appearing more superior to me as they appear more able than me socially. I can't help that, but it's taken many years to realise my social skills are never going to be perfect. I feel they're now good enough though to get me through life.

You've also probably gathered by now that I don't like hanging out in groups. I find it very uncomfortable mainly for the reasons mentioned above. I even find church difficult sometimes for this reason. I find meals out awkward as I've also established. I even find meeting with friends awkward if they decide to bring along a few of their friends. I really don't like it when that happens. I arrange to meet a particular person so that's what I expect. When I turn up and there's a group present I just want to turn around and go home. I'm nice though; I'll say hello, set a target of a few sentences, and then job done. I aim to feel that I've done just enough not to have come across as very quiet and shy. I'm not a shy person at all; I just sometimes like to choose when to speak. At the end of the day, particularly now I am suffering from M.E., speaking uses energy, and I prefer to use my energy very wisely.

Sometimes though the barriers will come down when someone mentions something involving a special interest of mine such as a football score; I'll go off on a tangent and I can't really stop. When I've stopped talking I'll take in a breath and think "Brilliant, that's my conversation sorted" - it won't look funny if I don't say anything for another 5 minutes or so.

Whilst we're talking about social outings, I'm going to mention the cinema. I don't really see the point unless it's because someone else wants to go. It does mean that I don't have to speak for the whole movie, but all I'm thinking about is what I'm going to say to that person after it's finished. I won't take anything in either. I much prefer a TV series in a quiet environment.

Relationships

As a rule, I generally don't talk about things like this. I'll deliberately be very vague when someone asks me about these matters. I've been hurt a lot in the past, and been taken advantage of, so this is a subject I keep close to my heart.

If I told you about my past experiences then your expressions would be a mixture of shock and laughter. Not me though, I don't have expression, obviously. Due to my gullible nature of not being able to interpret things how they should be interpreted, I have gotten myself into some ridiculous situations.

In relation to relationships and dating, you would never see me approaching someone. I might give a little smile but if they start to play games then I can't be bothered. I only really smile because I think it's polite. If you get a smile from me then you should feel quite honoured.

When I've been in nightclubs and girls have tried to get me to dance, I'm probably the only guy who doesn't like it. Without sounding harsh, how much have they had to drink? Where have they been? How many others guys has she been kissing? I can count the amount of women I've kissed on 1 hand, and that's through choice. I'm extremely picky. What's the point in dating someone who you just quite like? I admit I've made some wrong decisions but I've learned from them. I don't like it when someone grabs my arm and tries to get me on the dance floor. I must look like a right Scrooge when having a wrestling match to try and prise my arm away from them. I like to get to know someone a little more before they touch my arm.

I've always got on better with mature women. I'm talking about 20 years my senior here. I honestly don't think age matters and if 2 people want to make a friendship or a relationship work then they can. At the end of the day, with all these illnesses flying about, life is short. I'd rather spend 40 years with someone I truly love than 60 years with someone I just think is Ok because they're a similar age to me. I once tried dating someone a similar age to myself and they had the personality of a fish. In fact, I think I would have got more conversation from a fish... and I thought I was the one who had social difficulties. If it's me who's taking the lead then you know something isn't quite right.

I find mature women more understanding, more attractive, and I like someone with a bit of life experience. Sensible when needs be, showing a genuine interest in me and what I do have to say, and who has been through enough to know what they want... or indeed what they don't want. I do actually know some women twice my age though who are just as immature as some 15 year olds.

Back in the day, I was just pleased to get attention. I

had a very mixed mind. These days I would never date anyone with a peculiar job occupation, anyone who's going through a divorce, or anyone who has a drink problem... honest... but back then I got attention I wasn't used to so none of that mattered.

I've always stuck to one principle though when dating. I've always stuck to my morals. Women appreciate the fact that I don't meet with them due to lustful intentions but at the same time are bewildered and relationships have always ended due to us looking for different things.

I can be judgmental at times and I admit it's a weakness. There are always ways I can improve. I'd never date anyone for the sake of it. It takes a lot for me to become interested in someone as I'm extremely picky. I don't understand cheating either. Don't be in a relationship if you're going to cheat. It doesn't matter how much drink you've had. It really is that black and white to me. Lad culture gives the few decent guys that are around a very bad name. Even worse is when women adore these men.

I've never thought that I had a particular type of lady I would like but when I asked my mum, she answered straight away.

"You like make-up as it's a disguise. When applied in the same way it achieves a predictable result so you can anticipate the appearance of that person. The look doesn't change. It also gives the illusion that there are no flaws or imperfections".

Wow, that makes me sound really shallow doesn't it? I don't totally disagree with that but it's harshly worded. Personality matters most to me but I have to be attracted to the person too. So what if I have a type? I never enter relationships for the sake of it; I'm always in it for the long haul...

Now

I've learned several different ways of coping and have developed different ways of behaving over the years despite still being young. I actually think I've matured a lot more rapidly than the average person because of this. I feel I can now more readily relax in conversation and although the social problems are still there, to an extent, they're not half as bad as previously and I've learnt to cover up my flaws pretty well.

At the end of the day, I stick to my principles and that will never change. I feel that's the best way to be, unless your behaviour is viewed as unacceptable to others. Then it's a case of taking it on board and adjusting how you do particular things. I'm at the stage where I can function as well as most in a social situation, but still more so 1-1.

I like to have my own mind; I don't want to be a sheep unless it's for God. I don't follow people. Unless it's on twitter of course, then I'll follow lots of people. You get the gist. I have a strong mind...

I have totally accepted that I'm a little different, but now, writing this book, I feel this is the first time I can really express myself without being too bothered about what others think.

Wow, this has actually been a long section. I haven't given too much away have I? Not as long as 'School Shenanigans' though mind...

Chapter 6: Routine Madness

Routines are a big part of my life. I couldn't function without them. Everything I do involves some sort of routine. I wouldn't say I particularly enjoy them, I see them as more of a necessity.

Timetables

If I get anxious I get in a tizz. I have a timetable; it helps me to see what I have to do next, otherwise I get confused. I like things to be written out in front of me so I have a clear idea of how the day is going to go.

I find there's a definite pattern when I have a routine, I feel much happier. I feel much more content knowing I've been able to fulfil the tasks which are written on my list for that day. I feel like progress has been made. The only problem is my short attention span; this makes it hard for me to keep up to date with lists. My mind will run riot and not know what it wants to do. I'm stable but I can get overloaded if there are a few things on my mind at the same time. Rather than do things one by one I try to do them all at once and it's when I can't manage that I have a little meltdown. Just for your information, these little meltdowns are a lot less frequent these days.

It can be like that working out at the gym. I liked quiet gyms. I used to have a set list of exercises I planned to do and if a machine I wanted/needed was in use then rather than move onto the next piece of equipment, I would leave the gym because it wasn't part of the routine. That only happened occasionally though, but if I did have to move onto something else, I wouldn't like it and it would spoil the workout in a way. Also, the gym is generally a lot like routines to me. It's always best to change the routine once in a while.

Whilst I've been writing this book, bar appointments and other things that may have cropped up, I've had a new routine, which for this moment in time is good. Now I'm knuckling down with the nitty gritty, this routine has lasted for a few months.

Daily Routine

With my current health it's not always possible sticking to a routine but I'll talk about that shortly...

8am	Rise and shine/Eat
9am	Shower (need a lot of rest after breakfast)
10am	Coffee shop/laptop/write
1pm	Lunch time
2pm	Sleep
3.30pm	Exercise (if able)
4pm	Snack
5pm	Cup of tea
6pm	Sleep
7pm	Singing practice
8pm	Tea time
11pm	Protein shake
12am	Bed time

That's roughly the routine time wise but it usually all gets done. Times can alter though due to various things that may happen along the way.

I have just mentioned what a daily routine would look like to me, but now, I'm going to go into more detail and talk about it from a wider perspective. I find it a lot harder sticking to routines than I used to due to my health but as stated before that will be mentioned later in the chapter.

First of all, I find it hard getting up early but I try to make that extra bit of effort to do so. This is because psychologically it has a better effect on me knowing there is plenty more time in the day to get more done. I like to have my breakfast between 8-9am. For me that's realistic; I know if I get up earlier then it is a lot more difficult for me physically to get through the day. I like to have a shower after my breakfast but sometimes it's too much straight after breakfast with no chance to rest in between. Being quick in the bathroom for me takes around 40 minutes; this isn't because I like grooming myself but certain things take a lot longer as I have to do them a very particular way, like turning the shower hose onto the same setting or making sure I rinse my hair a certain number of times before I'm satisfied that it's washed.

Then between 9-10am I like to take myself out to a coffee shop to do some writing. My laptop battery lasts around 2 hours (not much I know but it gives me a time limit at least). Then ideally I like to be home before 1. That's because I like to give myself time for a coffee to digest into my system before lunch time. If I don't do that then I can feel pretty ill.

I like to have my lunch between 1 and 2pm. If everything goes to plan between 8am-2pm then I feel content for the rest of the day. These are the key hours for me. Physically, with my present health problems, I can't get through a full day without resting, so around 2pm I like to take it easy for a bit. By 3pm my lunch has had time to be digested and I may a bit of singing unless I have other plans. When singing the correct way (through the diaphragm) I have to make sure my stomach isn't full as I'm applying more pressure to that area. This can take a while but I feel sick otherwise. Things vary though with how I'm feeling on a particular day. Some days after 30 minutes singing I start to feel a little dizzy and tired. Between 4-5pm I like to have my Greek yogurt with cereal to prevent the starvation response. I take my food very seriously which I'll also explain very shortly. I have my own very specific food routines.

By around 8pm I'm ready for my tea and an episode of a crime drama. I usually have a couple of my pet rats with me as they are very good company. This keeps me sane. I find it hard to concentrate on television so I'll usually complete a few crosswords at the same time as I'm watching. I still take in just as much. Later on I like to have a protein shake, usually around 11pm, after doing 10 minutes of exercise. Again it depends how I'm feeling physically; more often than not it will get left, so this is something I need to sort out.

Overall, I like this routine. It keeps me occupied without exerting myself too much. It's ideal for a certain amount of time, but I like to change it slightly from time to time. My mind doesn't have time to properly wander until around 2pm and by that time I've already got a fair bit done. Saying hello to staff in shops is my idea of socialising and it helps me to think I'm not becoming a full-time hermit.

However, I often find that if things are running a little late (30 minutes or so) that it doesn't bode well for the rest of the day so this is a problem. Sometimes it works out better to leave the house an hour after my lunch as it 1) gives me time for the food to digest and 2) it gives me more chance to do stuff in the morning that can leave my mind later on. This has to be carefully planned as I like to have a snack at about 4pm though at a push it can be an hour either side if needs be. If I have an appointment of some sort (of which I have a fair few) then the whole thing turns into jeopardy. Things have to be done a certain way.

Bed time is a nightmare. My mind runs riot and I put it off for as long as possible. I know I'm not capable of switching off. I need to play on my phone for about an hour to give my mind a chance to wind down and eventually it will wear out and I will go to sleep. It's the one time of day I can't plan because it's so unpredictable. I tried taking sleeping pills twice when I was younger; first time it worked a treat but the second night it had no effect whatsoever.

Without having a routine my whole day falls apart. If one of my aims doesn't go to plan I find it hard to get back on track. It's often all or nothing which makes things hard work. I try to let nothing stand in the way of me and my routine. Some people might say "To get to my son/daughter you'll have to get through me first" but with me it would be "To get to me you'll have to get past my routine first" or something like that.

As you may have noticed, I like to get jobs done earlier on. If I leave them till later then all I'm thinking about all day is what I have to do. I can partly put my mind at rest if I get things done earlier on, but never fully.

Exercise & Dieting

You also may have noticed that I have a passion for exercise and dieting because it's good for your body and your health; but another reason these appeal to me are because they are a routine. You'll hear a lot of people at New Year announcing that they're starting a new diet and exercise routine in order to get that 'bikini body' but in reality most of the time it never works out. If I announce something then it gets done. I actually find it relatively easy sticking to healthy foods. I don't eat because I want to but because it's practical. I know what foods I need to eat in order to achieve my goals so I just do it. If I could liquidise my foods knowing it would have the same effect then I'd have no hesitation to do that but solid foods are a must when able.

I calculate calories and have a few mismatched foods together. Sometimes I just can't stomach certain foods, like peanut butter and more recently eggs. I like my food plain; I never have salt or butter on anything except the salt already in the food of course, that's why ready meals are a big no. I have an intense dislike towards them. I have potatoes plain and just about everything else as well. I have eaten the same food for breakfast most mornings since I left school 6 years ago. Porridge and banana in case you're wondering. I don't enjoy it much but it's good for you. I went through a phase of having pasta with sauce for tea every night for a few years and the same for 3 baked potatoes with cheese, ham and tomato for lunch. I get fixated on a certain meal because I know exactly what I'm going to be eating and there's no thought process involved when thinking what I want to eat. I want it settled in my mind so I don't even have to think about it. I don't like altering my diet because it changes my already planned routine and I don't like that. I am very picky with foods, just in case you hadn't gathered that already...

I'm not as bad these days, but at one time if I said I

would have 6 meals then I would; 6 because you never get hungry, and I would follow bodybuilder like meal plans. However, sometimes I would run late and it would ruin the whole day.

Some days I might only have had 3 meals by 8pm and stress that 3 more need to be eaten rather than doing without them. I would plan my mealtimes hourly or every couple of hours, so would then have to eat at 8pm, 10pm and 12am. I couldn't just leave the meals out because I would believe that I'd failed in achieving my goals, which at the time were putting on muscle as I'd always been slender.

It's similar with drinks too. I never drink juice or pop, always water. I don't like leaving the house without a bottle of water as I've worked out that every 30 minutes or so I start to get a sore throat

I do like going out for a coffee though but at times it's become more of a routine than actually wanting to drink the coffee. I can feel like something is missing if I don't have a coffee at a certain time if that was in my plan for that day. Well the coffee would be missing of course, but it's nice having something to hold onto like a cup handle. In a way it's like a shield when I'm in an inevitable awkward social situation. Whenever there's an awkward silence I can just raise the cup up to my face for a sip even if I don't feel like one.

It would only seem right now to add another little table in with my meal routine as I've done 1 for my general routine. I don't like to vary my foods due to reasons explained above, and yes there's 5 not 6 as I eat less than I used to.

Meal 1	Porridge and banana
Meal 2	Pasta/tuna/cottage cheese
Meal 3	Greek yogurt/cereal
Meal 4	Chicken, brown rice, tomato, spinach, feta cheese
Meal 5	Whey protein/semi-skimmed milk

Not ideal or the best diet in the world, but it's good on a budget, and most importantly it suits me. Every so often I will change a certain food but only when I'm feeling adventurous, which isn't often.

I've also started to add in juices which I'm having before breakfast to help clean my system. It takes away the guilt of failure if I haven't quite managed to get in my '5 a day'. My rat's like juice too so it's a win-win situation for all parties. It's psychologically good too which is very helpful when planning and sticking to routines.

Future

I always look to the future when thinking of and planning routines. You will notice a pattern. Singing, theology, diet etc., I see them all as part of a routine. Ironically I don't always enjoy my 'hobbies' but I do them because they're hobbies that will lead to a better future for me.

I have a rough outline of my routines for next year. They'll change a few times but will be noticeably similar to the ones mentioned. I alter my routines to accommodate a project if I'm working on one. At the moment it's this book. Next it will be my nutrition course/personal training website which I've been planning for a while. I like to make room for my theology too but that's a course I can take as long as I like with. These hobbies could possibly lead to a number of other things like more books, recording an album, who knows? Maybe I could preach to teenagers who've been in hard situations like myself? I'm hopefully opening up new doors.

It's not about making money or even becoming known. It's all about keeping my mind occupied and working towards something. It keeps me going. I can't be content if I'm not working towards something. Progression interests me. Everything is planned with a view to progress. I want to look back every year and be able to make a list of things I've achieved to reassure myself that it's all been worth it.

Changes

Ok, it all seems very organised and practical for me to have a routine, but that's only until a change occurs. I've skimmed over it but I find changes in my routine very difficult. Things like social events or something unavoidable like illness will cause change.

I'll use this as a chance to explain why I find it more difficult sticking to a routine now more than I used to. A lot of you will know I was diagnosed with M.E. in January 2013. The few months prior to that my health deteriorated and has since worsened, but at the same time it can fluctuate a lot.

The reason it's very hard sticking to a routine these days is because often I find it difficult even getting out of bed. Not because I'm lazy but because every morning my joints and limbs feel very fragile. The pain is sometimes unbearable so sometimes it's best for me to rest all morning to try and prepare myself for the afternoon. I can still feel like I've achieved something in the day if I manage to make a plan for the afternoon. I'm on a tighter schedule now but rather than moan about it, I work around it.

Fatigue can hit me bad at any time and is more likely to affect me after an increase in activity. I have to take this into account which means I have to plan naps. I don't enjoy naps but I know that they're what my body requires and I see them as just another thing to cross off on the list.

So taking all of this into account, I've had to find the right balance between having the illness and sticking to a routine which enables me to remain partly satisfied.

Now I'll explain more about changes in detail. What happens if my routine changes? I enter meltdown inside but keep a fairly calm looking face on the outside.

Why? I like to do things a set way and don't feel that things have been achieved if done a different way. I have my mind set on something particular so anything that disrupts that throws me. Instead of forgetting about a change, it will take over and I'll end up getting nothing done. If I try to continue with my other plans then that 1 change will just be playing in my mind for hours on end meaning it's very hard to stick to other things. I don't like that but I have to accept that that's the way it affects me. I tend to write those days off and look to the next day to get back on track. Monday's usually a good day as it's the start of the week.

I try to prepare myself for possible changes but always expect the worst. When someone makes an arrangement with me, I'll have it in my head that there's a 50-50 chance that the arrangement will actually take place. I've probably just met the wrong people but then I don't think you all need to hear anything more on that subject, for now anyway.

One of the things I talked about previously was going out for meals. I really don't enjoy it that much, mainly because it means I have to eat something different and I don't like eating foods I'm not familiar with. I view meals often being a more intimate romantic event which is another reason I don't look forward to them because as you all know by now that area for me hasn't been great.

For the billionth time, although I have a great need for routines, I find it hard sticking to them because so much runs through my mind. Others will change plans. They don't understand.

I'm not a big fan of Christmas, Easter or Birthday's either.

It's extra difficult over the Christmas period to stick to a set routine. Mainly because 'normality' changes. People have a break from work and they like to arrange to meet up. I'm the opposite as I prefer to meet up less during this time.

Religious-wise I love Christmas because of what it stands for, but other than that, I really don't like it. Why? There's a big change in routine. The same reason I don't like weekends. I much prefer Monday to Friday than Saturday and Sunday. My main priority on Christmas day is getting to church. Once I've done that I like to get back to my 'normality' as soon as possible.

It's for this same reason that I don't particularly like birthdays.

I play down my birthday as much as possible. I don't want to celebrate being a year older. I don't see why I deserve any presents just because I was born on a particular day; surely my mum should be given presents then because she's the one who gave birth to me.

I find opening presents very socially awkward too. I don't like receiving gifts from friends or partners because I've never had a friend or partner who's stuck around for the long run. I don't want to be reminded of them when I see their gifts so it seems better to me to not bother. I don't like it when people buy me gifts unless they're blood relatives though there's very few of them. If I had a kid then of course a present from them would be nice too, I've always wanted a little girl actually, but if I end up having a boy I'd be just as delighted. I'd love to have quadruplets so I could call them Matthew, Mark, Luke and John. If I don't have quadruplets then I'll have to get 4 male rats which would be a good substitute because they're less maintenance and I don't have to put up with a wife nagging away at me.

Basically, I don't function very well without some sort of routine. I think you get the gist now with how important they are to me to achieve my goals.

Chapter 7: Special Interests

This section of the book is going to be slightly different. There will be a fair few pictures as it helps to recreate memories and sometimes pictures speak louder than words.

I feel this is a very significant chapter when describing my journey with Asperger Syndrome.

For this section, I decided to dedicate 4 whole chapters to my 4 main interests. Why? Because they play or have played a big part in my life. I also think it will be interesting to show you in detail how deep my interests become. To get my point across, as I just mentioned, I will add lots of pictures to help you to understand more. Pictures speak louder than words, but only sometimes. I don't get catchphrases a lot of the time but that's a good one that actually makes sense to me. I won't go too much into that as I thought it would be a good idea to have a chapter talking about catchphrases and riddles in a humorous way... I hope.

When it comes to my 4 main interests, you can see that there is a very clear pattern. First of all, there's a chapter on animals as they've always played a big part in my life and so deserve a chapter, whereas the other 3 interests are ones that at certain points have become almost more of an obsession.

My first big interest came when I discovered wrestling when I was aged 9 years. When I started high school, football took over. I'm still a fan of the old wrestling and football but I've more recently become a big fan of music, and am particularly interested in singing. One interest tends to take over from another, though I still have interests in all of these 3, wrestling to a lesser degree though. There are clear patterns that form when comparing the 3 interests. Collecting and then gathering statistics is a big thing for me which I'll talk about in more detail later on.

Before I talk about my 'bigger' interests, I'm going to show you a few of my 'smaller' interests that are a lot more general. Things that have always been there but they don't take over quite as much as the main ones.

Numbers

I mentioned in the first chapter that I loved numbers. I have to work digitally; I have trouble even now telling the time from a non-digital clock. I like the look of numbers. I feel something is missing if there are no numbers on things. 1 example of this could be a clock with roman numerals; I don't like these as, to me, they don't look like 'proper' numbers.

I enjoy counting things. I like counting my calories. Making sure the balance of macro nutrients is correct. I enjoy working things out.

Money is another one too, I'm very careful with money. I like checking my savings account daily or my sales/income from elsewhere just to see the numbers. In my savings account I always have to round up the figure to the next 0. It can be a little costly once the interest appears as I then have to round the figure up again and end up saving more than I had initially planned to. Not a bad habit to have though.

I like it that my car works digitally too. Whenever, or if ever, I was to exceed 80mph on the motorway, I start to match the numbers between 80-95 (not that I go that high...) with previous Premier League champions starting with the season 1999-2000. I'll explain in a later chapter about my likes for particular seasons.

I've made a little table to show you how it works. The figures on the left are the total amount of points whilst the figures on the right are the seasons in chronological order relating to the teams in the middle column. Hopefully you'll make sense of it...

80	Manchester United	2000-01, 2010-11
83	Manchester United	2002-03
86	Chelsea, Manchester City	2009-10, 2013-14
87	Arsenal, Manchester United	2001-02, 2007-08
89	Manchester United (2), Manchester City	2006-07, 2012-13, 2011-12
90	Arsenal, Manchester United	2003-04, 2008-09
91	Manchester United, Chelsea	1999-00, 2005-06
95	Chelsea	2004-05

It keeps my mind occupied with figures whilst I'm on the road. I've always made a little table at the opposite end of the scale too. Teams that have been relegated are used when I'm going around 30mph. I wanted to go up to 33mph but there were too many teams to add in but you still get the basic picture I hope. The same rules apply as the table above.

11	Derby	2007-08 (traffic must be really bad)
15	Sunderland	2005-06
19	Sunderland, Portsmouth	2002-03, 2009-10
24	Watford	1999-00
25	Wolves, QPR	2011-12, 2012-13
26	Bradford, West Brom	2000-01, 2002-03
28	Leicester, Watford, Reading	2001-02, 2006-07, 2012-13
30	Derby, West Brom, Burnley, Hull, Cardiff	2001-02, 2005-06, 2009-10, 2009-10, 2013-14

You will see by now that in everything I do, numbers are involved. I could go on for hours and hours about numbers but the pattern is there to see. After all, I'm writing a book about my experiences, not mathematics.

Symmetry

Now this may seem a fairly peculiar thing to talk about under interests but I like symmetry and feel I need to add this in somewhere and this seems to be the most appropriate place.

I like all things to be symmetrical. I feel that if something isn't symmetrical then it can appear lop sided or uneven. I have 6 ear piercings and every single 1 is symmetrical; 1 at the top of each ear, 1 in the middle and 1 at the bottom. Symmetry is also maybe the reason as to why I love animal's faces so much. No matter how hard you look, everything tends to be even unless they have blotches... or a botched operation. It's also why some might think I come across as vain; I look in the mirror and if something isn't symmetrical then I don't like it. There are certain aspects of my features I can't change and I've found that hard to come to terms with to be honest. I'd say it stems more from insecurity than vanity.

I realise I have a certain 'type' when it comes to the opposite sex and again it all comes from symmetry. Some may say I have very particular taste but I like a symmetrical look and if that means heavy makeup, then so be it. I seem to be oblivious to the impression it may give out to others but that's my taste; the fact that I also take personality very seriously could also be another reason I haven't had much luck in this area. I'm fussy and I'll admit that I don't like being this fussy. I don't like having my hair to one side because it feels uneven. If I have a scar then I want one both sides. Whether you like it or not, I will know every single facial flaw you have. I sometimes forget that make-up can cover that up because I can't see it. I don't like to study people's faces but, like with everything, you can sometimes be drawn in to certain things.

I like to wear makeup myself at times. It's a way to express myself without saying anything. I like the glam look and it doesn't faze me and there's also a lot of symmetry involved. Despite previously suffering from a lack of confidence, I was always comfortable on photo shoots when I was able to prepare and 'glam' myself up. It was also 1-1, which as I've explained before, is more comfortable for me. I wasn't at ease attending shoots with anyone else. I once had a boob pressed against me. Some people may think I'm crazy but I didn't like that at all. It felt like a mini periscope prodding against my pectoral.

TV

TV is another interest of mine and it's becoming more obvious that this is a chapter where I add random things in when I can't find anywhere else that they may fit.

I'd never really watched much TV until recently and even now I very rarely watch live TV unless there's a football match on. I prefer to record things to watch later. I particularly like if there's a new 'gritty' drama on.

Unless it's football, I don't like watching TV on my own because I never understand what's going on. I need someone to watch with me to explain certain bits that are happening. The only person I do this with is my mum as it's not exactly something I felt I could say to my friends as they would just laugh. There are very simple things I don't understand, but

if it was explained in a different way, then I could.
I always like to watch a good TV series. I love crime
dramas. I used to want to be a policeman or a prison
guard so I liked to imagine myself in these types of
roles. I'm very predictable; you can look through my
shelves and there'll be a line of crime dramas.
Everything is in alphabetical order in different
sections when it comes to DVD's and VHS tapes. I
have a comedy section, films, TV series and sports
sections. Even the categories are in alphabetical
order. It's the same with CD's. Very formal and well
organised.

I can also develop special interests for certain actors
or sports players. When this happens, I like to make
a collection of TV series they've been in or
memorabilia if it's sports players. There was a
particular occasion when I used to watch Coronation
Street. There was a character called Alec who was on
the show before I started watching it. Another
character on the show mentioned his name and I
had to find out more. I then bought a VHS tape of a
particular episode of the show so I could see who he
was. I decided after that that I wanted him to return
to the show so I got my dad to write him a letter
asking if he was planning on returning to it. He said

no but I got a signed picture with a nice letter to go with it that was put into a frame. I quickly lost interest after that and have no idea where the signed photo and letter ended up.

I like stand up comedy to an extent, but not for the reasons you would think. I find it entertaining in the way that the 'jokes' made I don't find very funny, but I see the logic in them. It's basically saying what I'm thinking although I don't think that's funny. I went to a friend's house and watched a show years ago and he said there was no way I could sit through the whole thing and not laugh. I'd be in stitches. Stitches? Laughing too hard your insides would fall out so you'd need stitches? I cracked maybe 1 or 2 smiles because I felt under pressure to do so but I never willingly laugh. It's always thought out.

Collecting

I have always loved collecting things. I like to have complete sets of whatever I have. It's not worthwhile having something if I can't have the full set whether it be Mr Men books, crime dramas or McDonald's Happy Meal toys. Those Happy Meals were a big thing for me; not because I enjoyed eating them (but

I did) the attraction was the toys I would get with them. Quite often I'd go to the counter and ask if they had a particular toy and offer money for them without having the food. In 1999 they had Snoopy dogs of the world. It was an absolute nightmare, there were dozens of them. I never quite completed the set but I was only a few off. I even asked to have the big poster on the store window and wanted the toys in the same order as they appeared on there. Every time I think of a country I have a picture of a snoopy in my head, even now. The only reason I know if a country is generally cold is if Snoopy had his winter gear on. A year later they had bigger Snoopy's to collect, in various costumes, and luckily there were only 12. I managed to get the whole set and still have them to this day sitting somewhere stored away in a safe place.

I liked sticker albums too, although they left me on the verge of bankruptcy as a child. I'll talk more about that when I talk about football as most of my albums involved that. Playstation games were another big interest. I liked seeing them lined up on the bookshelf... but only on 1 condition. The side of the cover had to be black. It was a nightmare when my mum bought Crash Bandicoot 2. It had a silver side. It didn't look in place so I wouldn't play it for a while. I didn't want it with the other games because it was different. Having a silver case meant it was platinum but I wasn't bothered. Black cover or no play. I went into a games store once with my mum to spend my Christmas money and asked the guy which games he recommended. I think he thought I was subnormal when I said I only wanted games with black sides. He said "It's a good game"... but I wasn't having any of it. It's the same with the TV series I was telling you about. I have to own all series otherwise they look out of place on the shelf. Complete sets or nothing.

The Big Ones

Now let's move onto the big interests...

The first big interest I am going to talk about is animals but the next 3 share a very similar pattern which I'll explain now.

My first big interest came when I discovered wrestling in primary school; **I enjoyed the sport but became more fascinated with certain figures and statistics whilst forming various collections.**

My second big interest was football which took over from the wrestling. **I enjoyed the sport but became more fascinated with certain figures and statistics whilst forming various collections.**

My most recent big interest is singing. **I enjoy it but have become more fascinated with certain figures and statistics whilst forming various collections.**

The pattern is self-explanatory and throughout the next 4 chapters you will see just how extensive certain interests can be.

Chapter 8: Animals

Animals are fascinating. I love them. In many ways I actually have a more solid connection with them than I do with humans. There are so many reasons for this but here I'm going to give you 10 very quick ones. 10 is a good number and the sub headings will be written just above so I only need 10 spaces across this table... not 11.

Animals	**Humans**
Always understanding	Sometimes understanding
No explaining needs to be done	There's usually need for an explanation
They love you for who you are	There are often conditions attached
They're cute however rough they look	Make up is often needed
There's always a way of getting around them	People can tend to not let things go easily
They'll lie on the end of your bed	They try to take up 3 quarters of your bed
They appreciate it when you feed them	There's often a criticism or complaint if something is burnt
They're very loyal	If someone better comes along they might go
They don't care how rough you look	They can be more critical of your appearance
Always pleased to see	Moan if you're 10

you	minutes late

You get a rough idea above. I would struggle without the presence of animals.

When I was younger I had 2 rabbits, Sooty and Sue. My mum overheard me talking to them one evening about when I was about to change schools. I can't remember what I said exactly but it gets the point across that sometimes it's easier for me to communicate with other creatures. Generally, I feel I can trust animals more than I can humans. That leads me to growing closer bonds, because animals never lead you on. They might not be able to talk but that's not always necessary. They understand a lot.

I love the features on animals. If they have big boggle eyes or a very odd feature then I'll instantly be drawn to them whereas I might not feel the same if those features were on a person. Sometimes I like to talk to my animals if I feel nobody else is listening to me or if I want them to know something which I feel is important. There's no pressure of having to make conversation though. When they look at you I don't feel any judgment is being made. They don't care if you make mistakes. Being around animals keeps me sane; it makes me feel more comfortable. I connect well with them. I know that animals can't always express themselves as they can't talk and to an extent I know how that feels. I can handle animals and I don't mind them touching me. I like the texture; it's quite therapeutic stroking an animal. There are many more things I could say but I think I've made some pretty good points.

Twinkle

I love all animals but I have a special connection with rats. Before talking generally about rats I feel I need to add a little section about Twinkle. She was very special. An inside joke meant she was always called 'Freckle' to me or 'Freck' for short. Why? She had a freckle on her cheek. It's very logical. I was a little downhearted when I found out the other 2 rats had freckles on their cheeks too though.

Why was twinkle so special? There was a connection. I really felt she understood me more than any other animal I've ever had. She knew when I wasn't feeling very well. She'd stay in my bed when I could hardly move and not wee once. If she needed a number 2 then she'd find a little corner and not make a mess. I didn't like the other 2 in my bed because Lucy bit any wires she could find (like my electric blanket) and Daisy tried to have a little nip at some sensitive areas. Daisy waited until I was asleep and then she'd stand up at my face and pull my glasses down enough for her to nibble my eye lid. It always woke me up; just a little warning because I wasn't paying her enough attention. Fair enough. Twinkle sometimes went down my top when I was lying on the couch and went fast asleep. She did this for a World Cup game. She'd pop her head out every so often to keep tabs on the score but it wasn't a very exciting game so she went to sleep.

Twinkle had intense rituals and interests. She would store the rat food in particular places. If she had a little treat like pasta or cake then she would store them in separate places, never mixed together.

She loved routine and was always waiting at the same place at the same time of day to come out and sit in my hood. I once made some protein cakes and they turned rock hard. I gave her 1 and she fought tooth and nail to get it up the ladder in her cage so she could store it where she wanted. She wouldn't let go. It went up and down the ladders despite being twice the size of her. Eventually, after a lot of hard work, she succeeded. She stored an avocado stone in the hammock once and I found it a month later. I used to have BBQ's in the summer and she stored bits of beef burger in her igloo. I find it fascinating. She made beds out of chip boxes and toilet roll tubes. She should have been presenting Art Attack.

I think if Twinkle was a human, she would have Asperger Syndrome. I'll give you a few reasons as to why I think that. Having said that, why can't rats have Asperger Syndrome?

First of all, her certain rituals and routines showed lots of autistic characteristics. She had a very vivid imagination too. I felt that she was the outsider with the other 2 rats she lived with because she was a little different, but I understood her completely. She wouldn't let the other 2 eat their food before she had stored it. It's like if your mum comes home with the shopping and you start to tuck into something before she's put it away in the cupboard, so I can understand Twinkle's frustrations.

She was also very obsessive in everything she did. She was quite possessive of me actually which made me feel quite honoured. She was content but everything had to be done in a particular way.

Rats

I've mentioned most things now with regards to rats but it's mainly been about Twinkle so I'm going to be talking more generally now.

If I feel like I'm not up to talking to people then I like to spend time with my rats. Some people talk to their pets and to an extent I'm one of those but I have to keep it realistic. I will tell my rat's things I think they'll understand such as if I'm not feeling well or I'm a little fed up. Their reactions to certain things I say prove to me that they do understand. They're my best friends. They never let me down and they're always there for me. I've never had a close friend who's done those things so the rats in their own way have been very special. If I'm tired then they will stand up at my face and lick my eye lids to stop my eyes from being sore. If I have my head down on the pillow and I have no energy and they sit on my face then they're protecting me. If they try to wash my teeth then I obviously need to brush my teeth. If I make them something nice to eat they'll lick my finger as a sign of acknowledgement that I've made the effort. Some would get annoyed if they bit holes in their clothes and whilst it's not practical, and I have to be careful what I wear, I know that they're only making air holes for themselves if things have gotten a little 'windy' or it's a bit stuffy. It's the same if they 'mark' me. In their minds, they're only trying to show that they consider me as one of them. People would say it's dirty and they're horrible but let's think about what their intentions are. They can be toilet trained after all. It's good when we consider other people's feelings so why not animals? Why can't they have good intentions? People think they're horrible and that they bite but they only do that if they're scared, I've never been bitten, and they're very sensitive souls.

As well as my original 3 girls, I also adopted Gracie, Mags and Pumpkin. They needed a home. I didn't really have the room but I felt so sorry for them. I've never seen animals so grateful. They would lick me like a dog and cuddle up on me and go to sleep. Mags and Gracie both reminded me of Twinkle. Mags likes storing. She'll store a few chips in the litter tray, a few more in the igloos and a few in the hammocks. They're not as organised as Twinkle though. Twinkle would have been a great shelf stacker at a supermarket.

Unfortunately though, by the time this book is published I will be rat-less as they've all been very unfortunate with their health. Numerous operations have had to be performed and some of them have had cancerous tumours, a very common thing with rats unfortunately. I'd like to say RIP to Daisy, Lucy, Twinkle, Gracie, Mags and Pumpkin.

I'm going to pay a little tribute now and show lots of pictures I've taken within the past few months to show you what we all get up to:

(L-R: Daisy, Twinkle, Lucy)

(L-R: Gracie, Mags, Pumpkin)

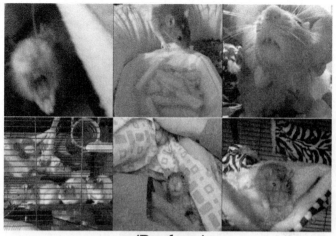

(Randoms)

(More randoms)

Cats

I like cats too but they're more solitary creatures.
They're very nice to look at because they're
symmetrical, and you know how much I like
symmetry. Just look at these faces:

(L-R: Nancy, King, Smokey, Zoe, Blitzen)

Their eyes, ears, mouths; it's symmetry at its finest. Blitzen is nice until you see his leg. He has a very unsymmetrical blotch on it. I want to tipex it out or dye it. I'd better not though.

Even Leo, a stray cat that we feed, who's 15 years old and had no home for 2 years, looks symmetrical and scrubs up better than most people...

Cats can annoy me though and it has taken time for me to get used to them. I think that's because they share a lot of autistic traits and sometimes characters who are very alike to yourself can come across as annoying. It makes me realise that I can be a little bit irritating to others at times. When both people share the same traits it can be hard to get along as there's no variety. There's no give with things like routine. I did a bit of research recently on autism in relation to cats and I feel there's a strong case for it.

Cats are very picky, and have sensory issues too. It takes a long time to gain trust from a cat. I feel that myself and our cats feel like we don't have to make the effort to not appear rude to each other because we're on the same wavelength.

I would say that my cat King is a prime example of this. He follows a strict ritual day in and day out. I have to make sure I shut my door at night as he will wake me up at 6am every morning asking for his dinner. It's always 6am and it's become a bit of a problem as my door isn't a very good 1 meaning he can hook his paw underneath and shake it a little to make a noise. He knows it gets a reaction as it wakes me up.

After he's had his food, he has to go out. He won't settle until you open the door for him no matter how long you leave it. Every time he comes home again he asks for a treat and won't leave you alone till he gets one. He also likes to have his second meal at 5pm but will ask for it before if he thinks he can get away with it.

He lives with our 4 other cats but hasn't formed any close bonds with any of them in particular. He is very much a loner. He'd rather follow his routine than make friends. His mind is never at rest and although I think I'm a lot better behaved than him, I can see a few similarities between the 2 of us.

As I did with the rats, I'm going to add in a lot of

recent photos of the cats as I just love looking at pictures of them. In this case, I think pictures definitely speak louder than words. From a few pages back you'll know who's who so I don't need to explain again.

Before I do that though, who does Nancy remind you of? She's very antisocial with humans but she photographs nicely. She has a bit of a turnip head though like a certain former England football manager. I like it when animals have heads shaped like vegetables.

I hope you enjoy looking through these pictures as much as I do. You may wonder why there aren't more pictures of King but that's because he doesn't like having his photo taken. Here's what he thinks to that:

Other Animals

If you know me personally then you'll know how many pets I have. I have however been having a bad run and that number is decreasing fairly rapidly each month at the moment. Here though I'll briefly take you through my other animals and my views on them:

(Malcolm)

Malcolm is a guinea pig; his ear is like a small piece of crusty bacon. It goes red when he's stressed, like an alarm. That's my way of understanding his needs. If his ear's bright red then it means he's having a hard time so I comfort him. He gets stressed very easily just like I can at times.

(L-R: Rocky & Bullwinkle)

Malcolm was adopted as a friend for Bullwinkle (above) after his friend Rocky died just 8 days after we got them. Bullwinkle passed away a few months ago after having a fit 1 evening.

(Harvey)

Harvey was a giant rabbit who recently passed away. He was a very loyal family member. He found it hard to express himself like myself. He is much missed by the whole family.

I could add more on smaller animals like gerbils, hamsters and budgies but I'm only sticking to ones I've connected with most to make it more readable as there are already a lot of photos to absorb in this section.

I'm going to finish this part of the section off with 2 very special dogs called Katy and Casey.

(L-R: Katy, Harvey, Casey)

(Katy & Casey)

I prefer dogs to cats despite living with more of the latter. Dogs are more faithful in my opinion and a dog has filled that void of having someone loyal in my life. Casey never liked sleeping upstairs but she wouldn't leave my side when I was suffering badly with depression a while ago, and she slept in my room with me for a few weeks. She wouldn't even let me wander off even when we went out to the beach; she would stick by my side like glue. The fact that she didn't like being touched by people and had a few psychological issues of her own made my bond with her even more special.

I've had Katy I've had for over half of my life and she understands me very well too.

I'm not going to go into as much detail with dogs as I feel animals like rats and cats have more similarities to autism than dogs do which is what I want for this book. I will leave you with another picture to gush over:

(Katy & Casey)

I find it easy to get on with animals and there's an instant understanding there. I'm typically good at handling them and seem able to gain their trust quickly.

All of my angry thoughts go away when I'm with them and I prefer cuddling an animal to socialising in a public place. If I go round to someone's house then I'm usually more interested in the animal than the person them self.

Fantasy League

Statistics fascinate me, as you know, and in each of my special interests chapters you will find a lot more statistics than elsewhere in the book.

I'm going to end this chapter with another of my tables but this time it's a little different. I've combined my love for animals, football and figures all into 1.

Football fans will know what I mean when I say 'Fantasy League'. You create your own football team using real players from actual teams and have a set budget to buy the players. Usually, people would ask friends and family to join a 'mini-league' where you're competing against each other. The points each team gets depends on real results from the matches played each weekend. However, I don't like inviting my friends to do this. I am allowed to include myself however.

I need to have 20 teams to make it slightly realistic. This means I set up 20 different teams but I like to have set rules.

I've put the rules together in a table of 7x2 and 7 is a lucky number so I feel this is going to be a lucky season. Especially if Manchester United do well...

Rule	Why?
Animals have to have players beginning with same initial as them self e.g. Rooney for Rhydian hamster	It adds variety and very few animals will have the same players
Animals can only change players in January transfer window	Fits in with real times and is less time consuming for me (let's keep it realistic)
Animals starting with the same initial can't both have a team e.g. Katy and King	Read rule 1 – too many of the same players (so Katy is with Casey as they're both dogs)
Goals difference is divided by 10	Realism
Only animals are allowed	Having people and animals together would be silly wouldn't it?
Variety in names e.g. County, City, Hotspur, United need to be used for at least 1 team	Well that's the way it is in the Premier League e.g. Aston VILLA,

Just to explain the above in more detail...

I create teams for most of the animals I have but there have to be very strict rules. All the players have to have a surname beginning with animal's name. So Zoe the cat had to have players beginning with Z. Then if there weren't enough players with that letter then I would move on to Christian names. Poor Zoe, she will always have a nightmare squad.

I enjoy going through the players and feel a sense of achievement when a squad is complete. Certainly for Zoe. If there weren't enough players beginning with Z surname or Christian name then it would move to E for surname and so on.

I don't like to have to pick players myself. I like these set rules because it adds variety and makes it more interesting whilst also taking the decisions out of my hands. I've decided to show you a picture of the 2014-15 season table after 8 games. I like the number 8 and it's just enough games to see how things are going to pan out.

	#	Team	W	D	L	⚽	Pts
▶	1	Barry Town FC	8	0	0	304	24
▶	2	Katy & Casey County	7	0	1	321	21
▲	3	Dixie Wanderers	5	2	1	277	17
▲	4	Pixie Patriots	5	1	2	231	16
▲	5	Killer King FC	5	1	2	188	16
▲	6	Alfie and his Ants	5	0	3	289	15
▼	7	Queens Park Daisies	5	0	3	280	15
▼	8	Rhydler Villa	5	0	3	262	15
▲	9	Bullwinkle Hotspur	4	1	3	238	13
▲	10	Nunu Troopers	4	0	4	183	12
▼	11	Malcolm Midgets	4	0	4	179	12
▲	12	Lucy Lumps	3	0	5	247	9
▼	13	Silly Boy City	3	0	5	222	9
▼	14	White Tigers	3	0	5	202	9
▲	15	Mitey Fleur Albion	3	0	5	194	9
▶	16	Jumping Popcorns	2	0	6	218	6
▼	17	Gerbil United	2	0	6	211	6
▶	18	Harvey Hoppers	2	0	6	182	6
▶	19	Freckle Allstars	2	0	6	145	6
▶	20	Zoby Zombies	0	1	7	128	1

(Premier League Fantasy League 2014-15)

A typical person would look at this table and think that it's just a table, which in essence it is. However, I find it almost mesmerising. So many numbers to analyse. What does each number mean? Why is this team placed here? Is it close at the top/bottom? How many points are in it? Is anyone going adrift? Who's scored the most goals? All these questions race through my mind in a split second.

I actually have less interest in the whole thing once

the teams are set up; it's the process I enjoy because it involves a challenge as well as figures and statistics.

Chapter 9: Wrestling

Growing up, wrestling was a massive love of mine. The whole thing fascinated me. It was on a Friday evening when my dad accidentally switched the TV over to channel 5 and WCW (World Championship Wrestling) came on. I'd never seen anything like it before. I found it entertaining and really got into the story lines. I was around 9 years old when I was introduced to the sport and at that time, lots of youngsters were into wrestling but mainly the WWF which at that time was the more popular company. The difference was that my interest very quickly turned into an obsession. It took over most of what I did from then on.

I managed to channel my obsession for wrestling into numbers and statistics. Seeing lists compiled of how tall wrestlers were and how much they weighed absolutely fascinated me. No-one would ever dream of bullying them. I was drawn to the big 7 foot guys. I became obsessed with guessing how tall a wrestler was and making different lists which I'll explain shortly. I regularly used online calculators to predict how tall I would be when I grew older. I loved collecting wrestling memorabilia and I built up an extensive collection of wrestling figures and VHS tapes. There were many different aspects of this particular collection which really interested me. Things such as noting the number of matches in a particular event, the running time on the back of the tape (and comparing it to other tapes I had), the little number on the side of the cover and putting them up on the shelf in chronological order. I liked to try and make patterns between the different numbers I found and tried to read in between the lines... lines that probably weren't there in reality.

VHS Tapes

I soon became a fan of the WWF too. Their VHS tapes were more readily available than WCW tapes and there were more action figures were available. In actual fact, the wrestling was probably better too. It was during the year 2000 that I really became obsessed with wrestling so the majority of VHS tapes I collected were from that year, but I did have some dating back to 1999 too. I didn't really want to know much about it before that particular year and not much after that either. My obsession was focused on those 2 years. In 2001 WCW was taken over by WWF (much to my disapproval) and as a result I quickly lost interest in the whole thing. It also coincided with the fact that it moved over to Sky TV which I didn't have. It was shortly after then that I became a big fan of football which I'll explain in the next chapter.

During the years 1999 and 2000, I could tell you every single thing that happened in the wrestling world. I still remember a fair bit to this day, despite not having watched it for a while now.

It gave me a great sense of satisfaction seeing the tapes lined up on the shelf with the numbers at the bottom including the age certificate. I didn't like having too many '15' certificates, I liked the '18' ones as they were red and red had always been my favourite colour. Whenever I was watching a tape and saw a montage of clips from previous events, I had to find out what event each clip was from. This was before the internet which made it quite difficult. I'd spend months trying to locate certain videos. The HMV stores in Blackpool and Liverpool were my favourite places: shelves packed full of wrestling videos. Those 2 shops were the only reasons I ever wanted to go on days out. It also shows you what lengths I would go to fulfil my obsessions.

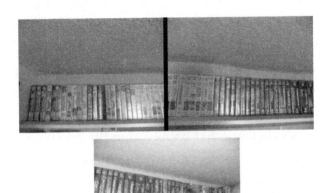

Above: It still gives me a great sense of satisfaction to see the tapes lined up on my shelves, despite the fact that I very rarely watch them these days.

There are some tapes in there from before and slightly after the time period that I was really into the sport, but I didn't watch all of the earlier ones, I just liked having them in the collection. There are very few I don't own from this period of time and they were typically hard to get hold of. I also have a few DVD's and recorded tapes too.

I loved my videos so much that I would calculate weeks in advance how much money I would have and if I could afford a particular video. They were around £14.99 on average and I got £2.50 a week pocket money. It showed my dedications that it took me 6 weeks so save up for almost 3 hours of wrestling action. Don't forget this was before I had the internet and sites like Youtube didn't even exist. I liked having something on the shelves to show my love of the sport. Here are a few calculations I made. I assume the ones at the top left corner are when my pocket money got upped to £2.99, though I can't be sure. It would have been £3 surely? I don't like it when things end in 99p. I like working in whole numbers, so if I want a pack of Haribo sweets I'd rather pay £1, not 99p (yes, they used to be consistently that cheap when I was a child).

(My most important childhood calculations)

Heights & Weights

Relating to my love of numbers, the heights and weights of wrestlers really interested me. At the time, I could tell you how tall every single guy in the wrestling industry was and how much they weighed. I used to calculate how much each wrestler weighed in stone by converting from pounds to stones, and then compare it to how much I weighed myself. Considering I was still in primary school, the majority of the guys weighed over double what I did. I got bullied a lot for being skinny and I wanted to be as big as these guys and do what they did. Kevin Nash and Kane were my favourites. I wanted to be 7 feet tall but had to make do with being 6ft3, which initially annoyed me because I wanted an even number. I would use height predictor calculators online when I was a teenager in the hope that I may have had a chance to be 7 foot tall. I even created my own books using note pads just to record how tall all the wrestlers were.

I used spare stickers from old sticker albums for the front cover.

This is a picture of the contents page in 1 of my books which shows you what I included in it: you can tell my handwriting had improved by that point...

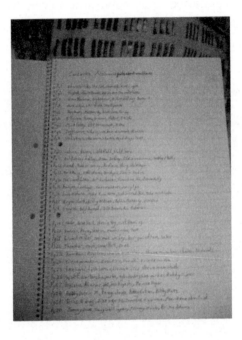

Quite a bit of time was spent creating this and I'd even thrown in a few facts about each wrestler to make it more interesting.

This next illustration is a page which demonstrates how the rest of the pages were laid out. Heights did vary slightly sometimes as it's been known that an inch or 2 is added onto certain wrestlers statistics to create a better character for the storylines.

I even used different coloured gel pens to make it look nicer.

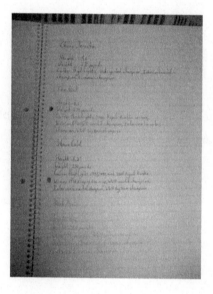

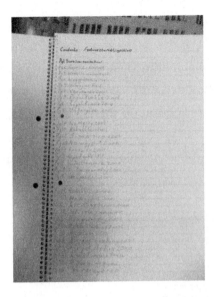

Above is the contents page for the other book which includes particular events match listings.

Below is a picture to show you how each page was laid out. Very detailed and organised, also a nice use of gel pens. It's a shame that gel pens were banned when I was at school. Children used to suck on them believe it or not. That's where my maturity comes in, I never did that.

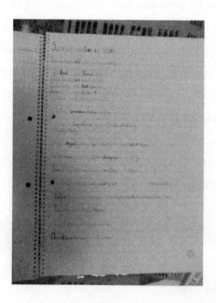

SBW

I took my obsession for wrestling to a new level with my vivid imagination. I decided to create my own wrestling company. I knew pretty much everything I needed to from learning about the 'real' wrestling world so I set out to create something of my own accord. My brother collected Sesame Street beanies at the time. I once saw them all lined up and something just clicked. I decided they would make good wrestlers. SBW, also known as Sesame Street's Best Wrestling, was formed. My creative mind allowed me to take my love for wrestling to the next level. Bert to me was like The Rock was to the WWF at the time. Rubber Duckie had no limbs so he had to wrestle against others with abnormalities like Oscar who lived in a bin, unless of course it was unavoidable in my mind.

And here are the culprits: (I never realized how much of a monobrow Bert had until now)

And here is the Championship belt:

And of course another picture just to show how much effort went into it:

Checklists were also made to make sure everyone was in order. It was like doing registration at school.

By now you must know about my love for facts and figures so it will make sense that these beanie toys had real life heights and weights, with an element of realism of course. How a rubber duck can weigh 10 pounds though I'll never know:

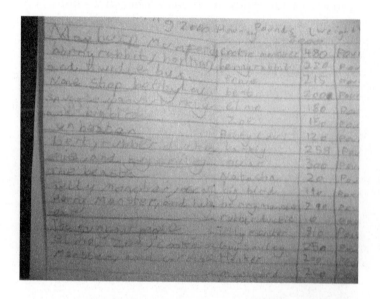

There was another page somewhere but I didn't want to bombard you with lots of pictures although with most of this chapter, it is the pictures that will do the talking.

Coming up are pictures of the 'events' that actually took place using our bottom bunk bed as a wrestling ring. I had lots of ideas but eventually they started to fizzle out. I pretended that Guy Smiley was Bert's dad because they were both yellow and it made for a good storyline. They faced each other in a 'chain match' in the December pay-per-view. The chains were the beads that my mum had bought to go on our Christmas tree. Some of the matches also had titles like they did on the back on the WCW tapes, for example 'David vs. Goliath'. Also, some of the dates you see in these pictures are made up; I did not actually do this after I'd started high school...

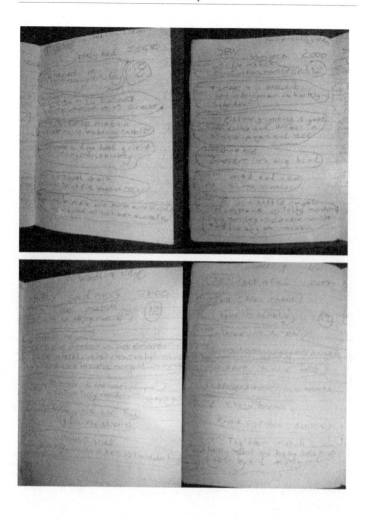

The reason I've added in so many pictures here is to show you just how much thought and effort went into this. It wasn't just something I decided to do on the spur of the moment 1 afternoon, it was all very thorough and carefully planned out.

BWM

In 2002 I decided to create my own wrestling magazine; I didn't like what was happening in the real wrestling world so thought I'd take matters into my own hands.

(BWM: Barry's Wrestling Magazine)

This is the front cover. I got my mum to write on the front as I accepted that her writing was neater than mine, at that time anyway.

There had to be a few pages dedicated to the heights of wrestlers, obviously. As mentioned before they did vary a lot as many of the stars are billed taller than their actual height, but I just loved the numbers anyway. I had to make it look vaguely interesting so I used a few different colours; I kept up a tradition with the gel pens.

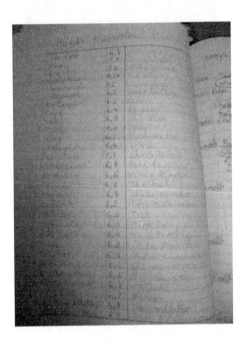

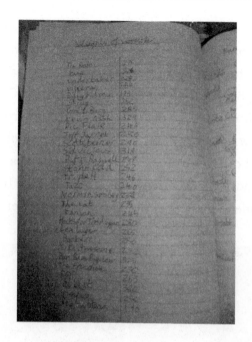

I wanted the magazine to be quite thick just like a normal one would be but I didn't have that much content to actually add in. However, I was mad on playing Smackdown on the Playstation so I would play out my own events and write down the results, also how long it took me to do this. It took hours and hours. I didn't particularly enjoy the matches after a few hundred of them but I had to get it done because I'd decided I wanted to put it in the magazine:

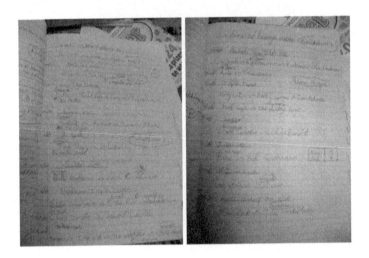

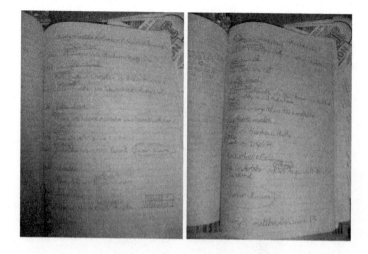

There are many more, though you will now have more of an understanding as to what I'm talking about. I spent hours on end doing these; I would even record them onto VHS tapes and watch them back, then try to make the matches look as realistic as possible. I even wrote down how long it took me to play out the matches on the Playstation as you can see. Sometimes I would create my own wrestling characters, though they had to be realistic and I would try to get the character to look as like me as possible, or how I thought I would look once I grew older.

Just to make sure I filled out the magazine with useless facts, I wrote a review of a randomly selected event I had a VHS tape of:

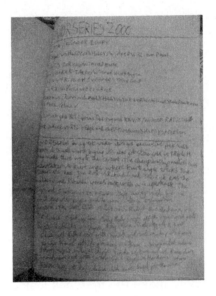

Another activity I enjoyed was playing with my action figures and using them to act out real life events. I had the whole lot though I gave away the wrestling rings eventually as they took up a lot of space; as the years passed I came to the conclusion that I wasn't going to play with them again now I'm grown up. This is a picture of the wrestlers. Many years of collecting:

Here is another excerpt from the magazine. The times shown are the real life times it actually took me to complete these tournaments; I took it very seriously. It would take up all my evenings and weekends.

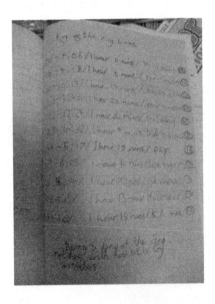

Other Projects

To finish off this chapter I'm going to give you an insight into all the other little projects I had created for myself around this time. I had a very creative mind.

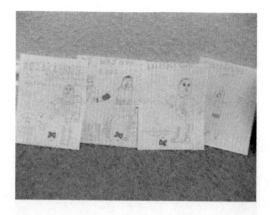

First of all, here are some scribblings. I made my own VHS covers for events that hadn't even been released at the time.

Below is what the back looked like for each cover:

This is an extra cover and you can tell I was feeling a little more creative as the gel pens made an appearance here:

Top Trumps were the 'in thing' at the time so I decided to make my own as there were no wrestling versions available at that time:

This 1 made me smile because of how random it was... an Easter card:

A birthday card:

And lastly, here are a few drawings of characters I had created that were inspired by actual wrestlers. I gave them all their own heights and weights:

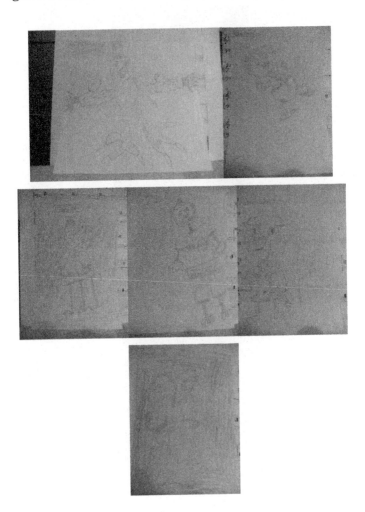

Above you can see the body stats.

So there you go, I'm sure you'll be fascinated with parts of this chapter but I'm not sure if that's a good or bad thing. If you think this is extreme then just wait until the next chapter...

Chapter 10: Football

Another big love of mine was football; in fact it still is, although not to the extent it was before. It wasn't until the end of the 2002-03 season that I 1st became infatuated with the sport.

Statistics

I was taken to see my first ever football game in January 2000. I didn't have a clue what was going on but Manchester United beat Arsenal 6-1. I thought Arsenal must be rubbish because they lost but they were 2nd in the table at the time. I got a programme at the game and was absolutely fascinated with it, mainly a particular page near the back. It was a results grid of all the football scores in the Premier League from that season (2000-01). I analysed all the scores and compared them to league positions of the teams involved. I was looking at this page for the whole train journey home which was well over an hour as there was a tram involved too. Shortly after I went to see United beat Coventry City 4-2. Again, I don't remember anything much about the game, but I later developed an intense interest into Coventry shortly after just because I'd seen them play at Old Trafford which I'll explain shortly. My worst memory of going to a match was in April 2002 – Manchester United lost 1-0 at home to Middlesbrough.

I got off the train and my mum was waiting. She told me that a puppy we had recently got had to go back to the breeder due to having bladder problems. I remember saying it was the worst day in my life. Rocky the Jack Russell. It was the 1st time I'd ever had a dog so I was devastated as he was only with us for 8 days.

Just a few months earlier, Manchester United had lost 1-0 at home to West Ham. I started to think I was an unlucky omen for the team as they rarely lost at home. The last game I went to see was when they defeated Manchester City 3-1 in December 2003. I remember more about that game as it was the 1st time I'd been after I became a lot more interested in the whole thing. I didn't like the fact though that the programme had changed; instead of a rectangular shape it was bigger and more square-like. I didn't like that because it didn't fit in with the other programmes I had at home.

After that I started going to see my local team Southport play. I made it a regular habit and often went alone which suited me. If I didn't get a programme I didn't want to see the game. I loved collecting which brings me to the next part of the chapter...

Collecting

I mentioned in the last part about my love for collecting programmes. I usually only actually read that 1 page in them which included the results grid though. A page with lots of meaningful numbers (to me anyway). Sometimes I would look at the fixtures page as well and compare attendances, then try to form patterns between the figures.

I loved collecting football magazines too but I ended up with so many that I eventually had to have a big clearout. It was hard but I knew I would never read them again, I just liked collecting. I didn't want anyone else to have them even if they offered me money for them as I didn't like the idea of passing on something that I had spent a long time collecting. I ended up chucking them out at the tip.

I was a big sticker album collector too and would buy packets of stickers with my pocket money. However, I wasn't really too interested in filling up the albums. In fact I never did actually complete 1. What I enjoyed most about them was reading each individual players career stats underneath where their sticker would be in the book. I liked comparing the stats and again trying to form some sort of pattern. I lost interest in purchasing the albums once the stats were briefer and didn't include the season by season figures. I only liked it when the stats were season by season as I viewed each season very differently.

As with the wrestling, I would collect VHS tapes, and also tape the TV shows though I'd never watch them back. I liked season reviews; I have on DVD too. I liked collecting so much that I even have 2 Liverpool season reviews which as a Manchester United supporter is a risky thing. I have a Chelsea season review and a Newcastle United season review. I even have Ipswich Town, Birmingham City and Sunderland season reviews. Birmingham and Sunderland were bought in an exchange shop and it was a spur of the moment thing (I still haven't watched them all these years later), but Ipswich

Town? For some reason I lump them in the same bracket as Coventry City. In fact Coventry, Ipswich and Derby in my head are a little trio with Leicester later entering the group. Why? I really don't know. Possibly because they'd all had a decent history in the Premier League before I really got into it. It's another of those things I just can't explain.

At 1 time I collected the little micro star figures which did absolutely nothing except look nice on the shelf. I only had room for them on top of a gerbil tank and every time I went to open the lid they'd all fall over and I very quickly lost patience. They ended up being given away after spending a few years in the shed. I quickly lost interest despite spending a fair amount of money on them. I would collect things despite not necessarily wanting what I was collecting. I bought them in bulk except for the first one. I liked Raul from Real Madrid; I bought him off e-bay with a maximum bid of £2.50. I later realised this bid was entered as £250 but luckily there were no other bidders. He was good but not that good...

I also mentioned earlier in this chapter that I developed an intense like for Coventry City after seeing them play at Old Trafford. Just the fact that they scored 2 goals against Manchester United and they were nicknamed 'The Sky Blues' which I liked. Sometimes our interests can't be explained and this is 1 of them. I'm scraping the bottom of the barrel trying to think of reasons I like Coventry City FC. I don't really know. Despite not really knowing why I was so attracted to them, I bought a DVD, a replica football, a watch, a sweatshirt and a badge. I never used the football as I didn't want to get it dirty which defeated the object of buying it; it now has a Halloween mask of a wolf's head over it so it ended up being useful. The watch I never wore and eventually it stopped working. I never wore the badge either and I never watched the DVD.

Games

I also like collecting games whether it is FIFA, Pro Evolution Soccer for the Playstation or Championship/Football manager for the PC.

However, I'd had to ban myself from playing these games. Mainly because it's the only time I can't really control my emotions. Throw anything at me and it's very difficult to faze me, but when it comes to games like these it's a weakness, and I've realised that after years of torture.

I'll start off with Championship Manager/Football Manager on the PC. Starting a new block would take over my life. Literally. Trying to get Southport promoted up the leagues always failed however many times I tried. I couldn't use the trick of not saving the game and redoing it because that would be dishonest and it wouldn't be realistic then. I always had to make it as realistic as was possible. In my mind I'm actually present at the games being played. I like the numbers side of it too and will make sure that all of my players get a game during the season just so I can read their stats at the end. When I was a teenager I used to sit at the computer with a notepad and pen writing down the whole line-ups for each game as well as noting down who scored in what minute. I'd never read them back but I liked keeping a record of what was happening.

I have great respect for my mum but I remember the one occasion where I completely lost it. She accidentally turned the PC off whilst I was in the middle of a game. I didn't speak to her for days and it took me quite a while to face playing the again. Hours of 'work' had just been deleted. I was so into the game that I would sit in school lessons thinking about what transfers I was going to make when I got home in that evening. My weekends were completely taken over too.

Unfortunately, I recently discovered a free app on my phone which was the latest version of Football Manager. I gave in to temptation but I have had to put a stop to it now. I took over 1,000 screenshots of final tables, player's stats and results. It always starts off with a very familiar pattern.

Just to show you a recent example (as all previous evidence has been eradicated) I'll show you a few screenshots of the pattern:

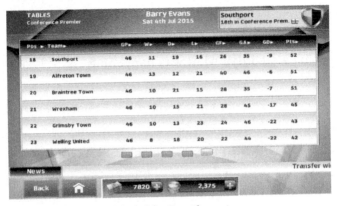

POS ►	Team ►	GP ►	W ►	D ►	L ►	GF ►	GA ►	GD ►	Pts ►
18	Southport	46	11	19	16	26	35	-9	52
19	Alfreton Town	46	13	12	21	40	46	-6	51
20	Braintree Town	46	10	21	15	28	35	-7	51
21	Wrexham	46	10	15	21	28	45	-17	45
22	Grimsby Town	46	10	13	23	24	46	-22	43
23	Welling United	46	8	18	20	22	44	-22	42

Finishing mid-table with Southport.

Losing out in the play-offs.

I'm very disappointed and would've stopped the game a while back if I'd have realised I didn't get a screenshot of the final table for this season. Again, losing out in the play-offs.

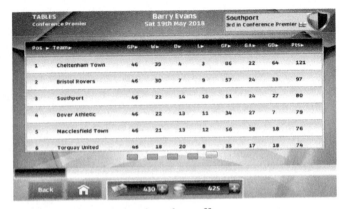

Again, losing out in the play-offs.

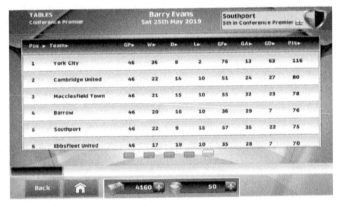

And again...

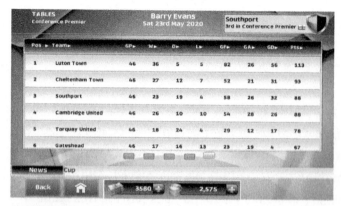

Pos	Team	GP	W	D	L	GF	GA	GD	Pts
1	Luton Town	46	36	5	5	82	26	56	113
2	Cheltenham Town	46	27	12	7	52	21	31	93
3	Southport	46	23	19	4	58	26	32	88
4	Cambridge United	46	26	10	10	54	28	26	88
5	Torquay United	46	18	24	4	29	12	17	78
6	Gateshead	46	17	16	13	23	19	4	67

And again…

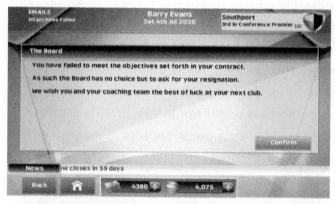

The Board

You have failed to meet the objectives set forth in your contract.

As such the Board has no choice but to ask for your resignation.

We wish you and your coaching team the best of luck at your next club.

And there we go, sacked despite being very unlucky. I take it all very seriously and end up in a mood for quite a while afterwards.

So there we go, pointless numbers, but I enjoy looking at these stats and analysing each individual number.

Now I'm going to talk more about Playstation games and actually playing football rather than just managing teams.

I remember getting a Playstation 2 for my birthday in my early years of High School. I loved it. FIFA 2003 was great. Spending hours buying my team and making sure all of the players played. All the time I wasn't in school I'd spend ages playing this game. I actually preferred creating my own teams in Professional mode and starting league seasons. I'd get a certain budget at the start of the season and would try to get the budget as close to 0 as possible. Like in real life, I wanted to make best use of the money. I would do it time and time again despite knowing which way it would go and what players I would buy. My eyes would get sore from playing on it so much. In 1 particular season, I was in the top 3 which was great. After that I had a big losing streak and so I didn't play on the game for a while after that. I remember shouting down at my mum and taking it out on her. It would wind me up even more when she told me I shouldn't be playing the game so much. If I lost out in an unlucky manner I would throw the controller across the room. It was like my whole personality changed: that's why I never buy computer games nowadays. As I mentioned previously, it's a big weakness. I never played any other sort of games, only football or wrestling games. I just wasn't interested in anything else.

League Tables

I really enjoyed writing this chapter. Do you know why? It's because I had a genuine reason to predict football results rather than through obsession. If you call out any 2 teams in the Premier League then I can tell you the home and away result for the past 2 seasons... that's 760 games. I don't study them but I love statistics, especially shock results. There has to be a certain pattern when predicting results however. I can't just make up the results. The results have to be based on previous results. I'll give you a few examples but if you still don't understand then don't worry because I doubt anyone else would completely understand it. It' difficult making predictions mid-season; it's always easier before it's started as it's a clean slate. I have lots of different ways of doing this but I'm never satisfied with the result. They will take me hours to do. They make my fingers sore and give me headaches but it's something I feel I have to do for some unknown reason. I just like creating league tables with new and old teams. It's strangely therapeutic just having numbers coming and going off the screen for a long while. I can think of other issues that are going on whilst doing these.

To show you how my Premier League Predictions work, I've made a list of the rules that apply for each format and why I've chosen them. Everything deserves an explanation. I will forgive you if you get bored or get lost. There has to be an element of realism included when predicting the results and I have to base the predictions on solid factual information that gives me something to work from. I'll give you an example: If you follow this then you're possibly as crazy as I am. You see, I've actually been having more of a life recently so these predictions were made a while back. I'm pretty sure I double checked them but you'll get the idea anyway. Let's get the party started.

What I've done is I've started from the very 1st game of this season (2014-15) and used this season's Premier League fixture list as a guide. Very often now there are games rescheduled for different reasons so I've gathered all the fixtures together week on week and changed them into alphabetical order. This is what I mean:

Man Utd v Swansea

Leicester v Everton

QPR v Hull

Stoke v Aston Villa

West Brom v Sunderland

West Ham v Tottenham

Arsenal v Crystal Palace

Liverpool v Southampton

Newcastle v Man City

Burnley v Chelsea

I don't like this because they all look muddled, so I have to change it to this:

Arsenal v Crystal Palace

Burnley v Chelsea

Leicester v Everton

Liverpool v Southampton

Man Utd v Swansea

Newcastle v Man City

QPR v Hull

Stoke v Aston Villa

West Brom v Sunderland

West Ham v Tottenham

See, they're in alphabetical order now. They look more organised. There are 38 match days in a Premier League season which means 380 games have to be rescheduled week by week in alphabetical order.

That's sorted now. How do we get the results? Believe me, I have many different ways. However for the book, I will give you just 1 example... although I could write a whole book on just predicting football results; I'm sure there are more interesting things I can talk about though.

I have a head start because I know off by heart all 380 results from the last time all the teams played each other at the top level. Let's take the first 2 fixtures from match day 1:

Arsenal 2-0 Crystal Palace
Burnley 1-2 Chelsea

There are 4 numbers shown here and 2 of them have to be replaced though only the 2 numbers on the left or the 2 numbers on the right can replace each other. This way, I can work out the most realistic results. There will also be a few surprise results as there's not much to work with, which is always likely in the Premier League. The above 2 fixtures will now look like this:

Arsenal 1-0 Crystal Palace
Burnley 2-2 Chelsea
The only other possible outcome was:

Arsenal 2-2 Crystal Palace
Burnley 1-0 Chelsea

That's not as likely due to the quality of the teams. Still with me? Well at least someone is.

Every so often there will be a few dilemmas. On the last day of the season, these 2 results occur:

Chelsea 1-2 Sunderland
Crystal Palace 0-2 Swansea

These scores stay the same because even though they look the same, the number 2 has replaced itself, if you get me...

Then there are scores like:

Leicester 2-2 Southampton
Man City 3-1 QPR

This means the 2 results have to be 2-1 and 3-2. In this situation, the team in the "big 7" always gets the highest scoring game. The big 7 being Arsenal, Chelsea, Everton, Liverpool, Man City, Man Utd, Tottenham.

The league table now looks like this (There are no goals for or goals against added at this stage because that would just take too long wouldn't it? I only do that when it affects a league position):-

		P	W	D	L	PTS
1	man city	38	27	7	4	88
2	chelsea	38	23	11	4	80
3	liverpool	38	22	9	7	75
4	man utd	38	21	10	7	73
5	arsenal	38	19	12	7	69
6	everton	38	21	5	12	68
7	tottenham	38	18	8	12	62
8	southampton	34	14	7	13	49
9	newcastle	36	13	7	16	46
10	burnley	34	10	12	12	42
11	stoke	33	11	8	14	41
12	leicester	35	10	9	16	39
13	swansea	30	9	8	13	35
14	west ham	33	9	8	16	35
15	c palace	33	9	5	19	32
16	qpr	33	7	9	17	30
17	sunderland	31	8	4	19	28
18	aston villa	33	6	9	18	27
19	west brom	29	5	6	18	21
20	hull	30	3	5	22	14

There are some fixtures left to be predicted but with some of them, I need a bit of direction as I tend to adjust the rules according to how the table is turning out. The obvious flaws so far in this one is that Hull need a lot more points and Burnley shouldn't get any more. That's because Burnley are favourites to be relegated and Hull aren't expected to go as far adrift as they are here.

It's all or nothing now. I pick 1 team out (Hull) and they have to amass the highest points tally possible from this position, obviously this will affect other results too because for each prediction, 4 teams are involved. I'll give you an example of this:

Southampton 0-1 Hull
Sunderland 4-0 Crystal Palace

The reason I couldn't decide this before is that I don't know how many points each team will have and I won't want any of them to break into that top 7.

After adding in Hull's predictions, the table now looks like this:

		P	W	D	L	PTS
1	man city	38	27	7	4	88
2	chelsea	38	23	11	4	80
3	liverpool	38	22	9	7	75
4	man utd	38	21	10	7	73
5	arsenal	38	19	12	7	69
6	everton	38	21	5	12	68
7	tottenham	38	18	8	12	62
8	southampton	35	14	7	14	49
9	newcastle	36	13	7	16	46
10	stoke	34	12	8	14	44
11	burnley	36	10	13	13	43
12	leicester	36	11	9	16	42
13	swansea	33	11	8	14	41
14	west ham	35	10	8	17	38
15	c palace	36	10	6	20	36
16	qpr	35	7	10	18	31
17	sunderland	34	9	4	21	31
18	hull	38	8	7	23	31
19	aston villa	37	6	10	21	28
20	west brom	32	7	6	19	27

Hull finishing on 31 points here means they're going to be relegated but that's not a shock to me and they've exceeded the 30 points barrier which is all good. If any team finishes below 30 points then I have to find a new format for my predictions. I don't like any team to finish below 30 points.

Aston Villa are now in a precarious position with just 1 game left. A big problem arises now as they have to win their last game to exceed the 30 point barrier. My first made up rule comes into practice now; a couple of scores have to be changed. In this instance it's:

Crystal Palace 0-3 Newcastle
Hull 0-0 Aston Villa

If those scores are changed so Aston Villa beat Hull, Villa now finish on 31 points whilst Hull finish on 30 points.

The only team now that have less than 30 points is West Brom. That's ok though because they have 6 games left to get over the 30 point mark. With maximum points, they can now finish on 38 points. The few results left now are predicted to be more realistic and to get a "nicer" looking table:

		P	W	D	L	PTS
1	man city	38	27	7	4	88
2	chelsea	38	23	11	4	80
3	liverpool	38	22	9	7	75
4	man utd	38	21	10	7	73
5	arsenal	38	19	12	7	69
6	everton	38	21	5	12	68
7	tottenham	38	18	8	12	62
8	stoke	38	15	9	14	54
9	southampton	38	15	8	15	53
10	swansea	38	12	11	15	47
11	newcastle	38	13	8	17	47
12	burnley	38	10	13	15	43
13	leicester	38	11	9	18	42
14	west ham	38	10	9	19	39
15	qpr	38	9	11	18	38
16	west brom	38	10	8	19	38
17	c palace	38	10	8	20	38
18	sunderland	38	10	4	24	34
19	aston villa	38	7	10	21	31
20	hull	38	8	6	25	30

In normal circumstances, I would have to find another way to predict the results and start from scratch because:

1. I don't think Man City will finish 8 points ahead of Chelsea

2. I don't think Burnley will finish that high
3. I don't like 7 teams finishing on less than 40 points

I'm not going to tell you about all the different ways I predict results but on average, it will take me 2-3 hours to produce 1 of these. It comes in phases. I won't do any for months and then all of a sudden I'll do about 3 in a day. It's a kind of stress reliever, typing numbers in my own little world helps to keep my stress levels down, though these tables themselves can produce a different sort of stress for me.

I don't expect that you fully understand what I was saying but that's the point. To me, it makes perfect sense but to the average person, they might get a little freaked out. I realise this. This is why I never talk about it. It's like having a bit of 'me' time.

Local Team

I'm going to finish off this chapter talking more practically about my love for football. In the previous chapter I could have talked about my time spent at a wrestling school but I felt it wasn't relevant to this story. There are certainly a lot more autistic traits involved when it comes to football.

I played in a team at primary school and my parents noticed that my reactions weren't as quick as everybody else's. I was a defender so I always wanted to wear number 2 or number 4. They were even numbers and looked good on the back of a shirt. At half time 1 game the manager pointed to the other side of the field and told me I may as well be standing over there as I was playing badly. Back then I took everything literally and actually went to stand where he pointed. I was upset because I didn't think I was doing anything wrong as I was only a kid.

Later on in high school I played in a local out of school team again as a defender. I was made captain 1 game which I was very nervous about because my communication was bad enough without this extra pressure. We ended up losing 13-0. I lasted 2 seasons but in the 2nd season I was dropped to the subs bench for a few games. I'd performed a lot better the season before because there were people in the team I liked. The 2nd season I was surrounded by people I didn't mix with at school and some would make fun of me. I had signed on for a 3rd season but ended up walking out as I felt inferior being with older players. I lacked the confidence to even shout for the ball.

I have a few medals which are still up on my shelf to this day. I got a medal once for playing a 1 off game for the older age group on my 16th birthday although due to there being no subs, I had to play most of the game with a bruised foot so couldn't actually kick the ball. We lost 9-1. In fact during my 2 years with the team we never won a game at all.

I always used to check daily for updates on other results in the league when it probably didn't matter to many other people. Again, I just liked seeing a league table in front of me.

Chapter 11: Singing

My latest interest which only started a couple of years ago, is singing; this chapter won't be as long as the previous few due to it starting fairly recently.

Starting

I've always been intrigued by performers who are a little 'different' and somewhat flamboyant. I like those who are controversial and stand out. I admire their confidence and watching certain performers has given me confidence in myself. However, I'm also very technical about my singing.

A couple of years ago I got in contact with a few singing teachers and also put up an online advert saying I wanted to learn how to sing like Adam Lambert and Freddie Mercury, not that I was aiming big or anything...

Anyway, there was 1 teacher who got back to me and he remains my teacher to this day. I always wanted to learn to sing but was always too shy and thought I was too bad to learn. On my first lesson I demanded that the house be empty except for all the animals. I was in fact terrible but I tried very hard with the basics, the main 1 being pitch which has improved significantly since I've been learning. I enjoy singing though I've still not sung in public yet, I've actually spend a lot more time studying the technical side of it...

Notes

You could have guessed that numbers would come into this interest somewhere. Here are the average voice ranges of different voice types though it can vary:

Bass – E2 - E4

Baritone - F2-F4

Tenor C3-A4

Countertenor G3 – D5 or E5

Soprano C4-C6

Mezzo-soprano A3-A5

Contralto F3-F5

The varying numbers do annoy me as I like things to

be set and factual. I like to listen to songs from vocalists who I like and then I try to match notes to within their ranges. I do however have a particular interest in high notes. I practice these a lot. The sorts of notes that metal vocalists would hit in the 80's. Despite my pitch not initially being great, I've worked on reaching high notes enough that I can guess approximately what pitch each 1 is. I read forums endlessly on singer's vocal ranges and then I listen to the high notes being hit in a song, mainly live performances. I like the notes G and A as they tend to be the most common ones I seem to listen to.

I also like the C note because they have different names:

C2 – Low C

C3 – Bass C

C4 – Middle C

C5 – Tenor C

C6 – Soprano C

I like it when things have names and I like it because I've practiced hitting the C note in all of these ranges. I've actually become more interested in notes than I have with the actual singing.

Vocal Ranges

Vocal ranges are of great interest to me. I tend to listen to music based on how talented I consider the vocalist to be rather than the actual music. I will watch the same clips over and over again. The same goes for songs. Rather than enjoy them, I study them.

I prefer to watch tutorial videos as opposed to live performances because then I am learning. I love the technical side of it. I have a little 'obsession' with what is called the head voice. I can lose a lot of people in conversation when I start talking about this. It is what metal vocalists use to access the very high notes but it can take several months, even years, of practice to perfect it. I try to find out where each singers 'vocal break' is and then compare it to my own. I have a naturally deep voice so I have a hard time singing in the higher ranges but it doesn't stop me from trying and I feel I have made a lot of progress with regard to this.

I like to read reviews that have been written based on singers vocal abilities and when they draw attention to every technique that the singer uses. I can spend hours trawling through forums discussing a particular singer's vocal techniques and qualities.

Learning

First of all, I do like to have a little dedicated corner for my music:

Here you can see the PA system.

Here is the stereo.

And of course here are the CD's/keyboard amongst other things, though this arrangement has changed slightly since taking these pictures.

I like to learn all the time but I find taking in information in the form of numbers and statistics helps me greatly, as you should all know by now. I follow the Jaime Vendera books because they're perfect for me. They're very technical and they have tables in which you can write down your own statistics whilst keeping track of your progress.

The book on the left covers everything you need to know about vocal techniques in detail, whilst the book in the middle focuses on everything you need to know about the breathing side of things. These 2 books have all the information needed when it comes to singing but it's the book on the right that I enjoy most. I'll show you why:

Raise Your Voice Diary
Jaime Venters

Week 27/01/2014

VSR	Mon.	Tues.	Wed.	Thurs.	Fri.	Sat.	Sun.
	x	x	x		x	x	
Falsetto Upscale-	G5	G5	G5		G5	G5	
Downscale-	G3	B2	F3		F4	G3	
Transcending Tone Upscale-	G4	G4	G4		G4	G4	
Downscale-	C4	C4	C4		E4	E4	
Full Voice Upscale-	A4	A4	A4		A4	A4	
Downscale-	A1	A1	A1		A1	A1	
Vibrato Pitch, Larynx, Stomach, Jaw-							
Non-Vocal (Buffings, Tongue, Pushups)-	60	60	60		0	60	
Advanced (Scream, Grit, Growl, Whistle)-	C5	C6	C6		C6	B5	
Daily Dose-							

Without understanding or even reading what's in this picture, you'll know that I get satisfaction from filling out the tables. These tables cover my highest/lowest notes in every possible way. I'm a perfectionist so that's why it will be a long time before I attempt to sing in public. I do get nervous when others listen to me and that's a barrier I have to work towards overcoming.

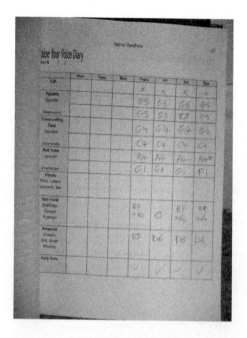

This is another picture showing you a record of my progress. I don't like tables that aren't full but I don't sing every day so I just have to put up with that. Basically, since starting out, my range has varied between C1-D6; though if we're talking about daily then it's closer to F1-C6, which is around 4 and a half octaves. Range doesn't matter though if you haven't got control or tone and this is what I sometimes struggle with.

Before moving on I will now show you a picture of my breathing progress.

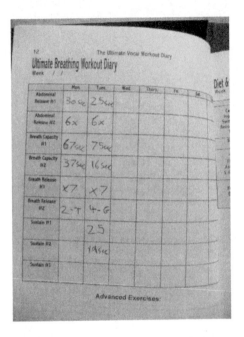

Basically, there are many different ways by which it is possible to hold your breath. How to perform these exercises are all in the 2 books I mentioned previously.

This is all very similar with my learning to play the piano learning too. I keep a set of tables to keep track of my progress. In fact, this liking of lists and statistics is probably the only reason that I watch the X-factor on TV, to wait for the end of series voting statistics so I can analyse them and look for patterns, as I do with everything.

Actual Singing

I've not actually talked about physically singing in this chapter so I'll do so here. More of my time seems to be taken up with the numbers side of things, surprise surprise.

I used to listen to opera when working out at the gym and I used to listen to clubland when trying to get to sleep. I have a strange genre style when it comes to these things and I'm also a little like that when it comes to singing. Some people would say certain aspects shouldn't go together. My lower range can sound operatic at times whilst my upper range can sound very rocky. I like to put my own spin on songs though I have an obsession with changing the key. This is a necessity really as a lot of popular songs are sung by tenors whereas I'm a bass-baritone. Maybe my stage name could be 'Barry Tone' or would that be too cheesy? Anyway, I typically find it easier singing women's songs as I can often sing them a whole octave below whereas it's too much of a jump to go a whole octave down when singing songs by males. It all depends on the comfortable range of the singer and I end up having this conversation over and over again going round in circles. You've probably not got much of a clue about what I'm going on about so don't worry because you won't be in the minority.

I sing lots of songs but I'm going to use just 1 to give you an example of the thought process behind learning a song...

I set myself very high ambitions when it comes to singing as the songs I pick tend to cover a very wide vocal range. I would say around 90% of the songs I sing are almost impossible for me to sing in the original key so I often have to go a whole octave below. Even my mum struggles to hit some of the notes in the songs...

Anyway, when I am learning a new song, I have to look at every single live performance of that particular song available on the internet. I look out for even the slightest pronunciation changes in each version, constantly thinking of new ideas.

I tend to do things the hard way because it's actually easier for me. I work very technically. Rather than just singing the song, I have to know what note the song begins on. For example the song might start on an E meaning I have to match that note on the piano thinking of that note rather than the melody.

I can't just listen to a song and add my own spin to it. I have to look into the technicalities first. When practising, I will often change the key to fit in with the high notes of the song. The rest of the lyrics come after that and fit in around the starting notes and the high notes. It can take me several weeks to master this and only then can I actually start to enjoy singing the song.

At the moment, I sing because I want to become a good singer, not because I enjoy it. Again, it's about progress. Planning for the future.

Chapter 12: Riddles/Phrases

First of all, I can take things literally at times...

Taking Things Literally

The World Cup 1998 was approaching and at the age of 7, I didn't really have any particular interest in football then. I remember my mum telling me about how England had won the World Cup in 1966. I said, "So we won the trophy?" to which she replied "Yes". I asked her where it was and started looking in all of the cupboards because she said that "we" had won the World Cup. I somehow thought that every household in the UK would have a World Cup trophy stashed away in the cupboard somewhere. That lasted for a few years before I gave up hope and thought we must have lost it or it had accidentally been taken to the tip as that's where missing items tend to end up.

My dad asked me if I wanted to watch the 1998 final between Brazil and France. I was very excited. I said "Where is it?" and he told me it was in France. I'd never been to France before. I was disappointed when the T.V. was turned on. I somehow thought that I was going to be flying out to France within an hour of him telling me. I thought I was actually going to the ground to see it. My only real memory of that World Cup wasn't the football, but actually the Frisbees you got with McDonald's happy meals. I can't remember the amount I lost that went into other people's gardens though. The rabbits seemed to like playing with them too.

During the 2002 World Cup England were playing Brazil in the quarter final. Brazil were favourites to win so I prayed that England would get through. It didn't cross my mind that there would be many Brazilian fans praying for their team to win too. How could both prayers be answered? I let that one go.

I used to get upset when I was younger because I sometimes had dandruff in my hair. A bit of a snow storm. I didn't know where it came from so asked my dad. He told me that 2 little birds called 'Dan and Druff' were flying 1 day and then landed in my hair so the white stuff was dead bird. I believed him for a split second. Actually, I think it was closer to weeks, even months. I was talked into believing it. It came from someone more knowledgeable than me so I thought it must be true.

Another time someone told me that milk makes your bones strong so I went out with a friend and bought half of a local shops supply of milk. I didn't realise it went off and remember being sat at the table forcing milk down me because it wouldn't fit in the fridge.

These are just a few humorous examples of how I can take things literally and still do to this day although not to the extent of the above examples. That brings me to the next part of the chapter which is about phrases.

Phrases

I think phrases contradict themselves or just generally don't make sense. Here is what I mean:

You can't find a needle in a haystack. I'm sure you could if you looked hard enough.

The early bird catches the worm. Does it? I don't get up early enough to find out.

Many hands make light work. They'd all get in the way.

Seeing is believing. It depends on what you believe in.

Better now than never. Why? It might bring you lots of unnecessary hurt.

There's no smoke without fire. Obviously, but why is that relevant?

All good things come to an end. Not always.

Actions speak louder than words. I've never heard an action speak.

You scratch my back and I'll scratch yours. You might not want the physical contact.

You can't burn the candle at both ends. You could try, but you just might not be successful.

Put it in your pipe and smoke it. Put what in your pipe? Be more specific.

I understand the concept of pigs flying, but when I was younger I would question as to why it wasn't a cow? At least with pictures and words, nothing can replace either one but with a pig, it could be any farm animal. Why don't you just say it's very unlikely? It would be a lot quicker than comparing the situation to a flying pig.

Something might happen once every blue moon. First of all, the moon isn't blue and second of all if there's never a blue moon then it's incorrect as the indication is that it won't happen often. Blue moons never happen. It's the reason I never liked the television show 'Catchphrase'. I couldn't read in between the lines. I can't now really.

Here's a little story relating to my main areas filled with ridiculous phrases that took me a long time to understand. It's half serious and half humour. You can work out which is which.

I'm not getting all defensive and I definitely haven't got a chip on my shoulder. What a ridiculous thing to say, a chip, seriously? Why don't you add a bit of sauce to that? It might stay once it sets.

First of all, I don't like anyone to be singled out and I've been bullied in the past so I have the greatest of sympathies for Gordon Bennett as I'm not quite sure what he's done to deserve all the hate he gets. I can relate to him. I guess you could say it takes 1 to know 1 when it comes to bullies but does it? I knew a lot of bullies so does that mean I was a bully myself if I knew them? People say a leopard never changes its spots. Well obviously, it's like saying a human never changes their skin. They could get surgery or a fake tan but it's still the same skin. Or let's put a new shine on an old penny. Why? Just get a new one. Well I guess you can't judge a book by its cover, but I think you can if the author hasn't bothered to put any effort into making a good cover. Talking about skin and appearance, let's talk about mutton dressed as lamb. I like older women who wear makeup so what's the problem? Don't be harsh on women making an effort with their appearance and don't be harsh on lambs, they're not very domestic but they're good hearted. I'm not sucking up at all and you may say that there's plenty more fish in the sea but why? It depends on what sea you're talking about; the river Thames or Southport beach? Bit of a difference... Second of all, why fish? I think of fish as being slimy, cold, wriggly and smelly.

I want someone to be smooth, warm, stable and pleasant thank you. I could always stop being awkward and break the ice but then why should a social situation be compared to ice? I could just go and live in an igloo which would probably suit me if it wasn't cold. You could always just burst my bubble but then I haven't got a bubble so you'd be wasting your time. It's not a piece of cake, I'd eat it otherwise. My humour might be dead as a door nail but then door nails are never alive to begin with are they? Maybe I could just lighten up and say that the grass is greener on the other side, but is it?

A lot of people say I'm mature and it's like I have an old head on a pair of young shoulders. No it's not. It's not my fault a lot of people my age are immature. Why would I want an old head, it would be a bit of a mismatch for my body.

As you can probably tell I've never really understood phrases. I use them a fair bit to fit in with everyone and others seem to find the misplacement of my phrases quite funny. Why can't people just get straight to the point? There really is no need for phrases, they're just confusing.

Riddles

I really didn't enjoy writing this part but let's get it done. I've deleted riddle after riddle from this text as they've all just been ridiculous so I'm just going to try and find some fairly common ones. I'm finding it hard because I find riddles very hard to explain but here goes:

Q: Poor people have it. Rich people need it. If you eat it you die. What is it?

A: Nothing.

First of all, poor people would have something whether it is clothes or a cup of coffee someone has bought for them. Rich people need nothing? They might be very lonely and need love. You could also eat poisonous foods and die.

I'm terrible at riddles and never get any right. I take everything too literally.

Q: I'm tall when I'm young and I'm short when I'm old. What am I?

A: A candle.

It's a well known fact that everyone loses some height as they age. What if someone has several knee operations or has to have their legs amputated? Why does it have to be a candle? I don't like candles anyway.

Q: What is the longest word in the dictionary?

A: Smiles, because there is a mile between each's'.

Why can't it be smiled? There'd still be a mile in between 2 letters.

Q: If I drink, I die. If I eat, I am fine. What am I?

A: A fire.

Fires don't have mouths and immune systems do they? And what if the drink is alcohol and someone has a very severe liver problem? They could still eat but die if they had a drink.

Q: If I have it, I don't share it. If I share it, I don't have it. What is it?

A: A secret.

Well there's no secret here, I detest riddles. Let's move on to the next chapter...

Chapter 13: Unlucky Number

You should know by now about my number
sequences, so rather than waffle on about something
I needn't say, I'm letting you all know that this is
chapter 13 simply to get the chapter number up to
15. The number 13 is a very unlucky number (look it
up if you don't know why) so this is the perfect
opportunity for me to add this here. I hope you
enjoyed it as I doubt anyone else will. Moving on...

Chapter 14: Q + A

So I write this chapter whilst being utterly exhausted physically though my mind isn't too brain fogged. I deliberately haven't looked at these questions beforehand as I feel the most honest answer will come to me straight away. I thank everyone who's contributed with some great questions for me and I've picked out a wide variety, so here goes...

How do you see/feel the world?

Difficult 1. My view has changed a lot since becoming a Christian. I was unsure before and never really knew what the point of life was. I now see the world as a platform to achieve lots without feeling afraid whilst doing it in a godly way. I view this as preparing for a better life...

Were you able to understand your parents when sometimes they were having a hard time?

My parents argued a lot when I was younger so over time I became used to it. If they wanted to be left alone then I couldn't understand that and I would persist. As I've explained, I've developed a decent knowledge of body language over the years so I'm more aware now of how to react.

How did your family cope with your diagnosis? Did they support you or back away?

My family have supported me. It was only really my 2 parents that knew in detail and it was my mum who persisted with getting an answer with regard to the problems I was experiencing. My mum wasn't sure how to deal with me in certain situations but over time we grew to understand each other more as the years passed.

How has your perception of your parent (s) changed if at all?

I used to be against my mum at times but I now realise she was always trying to help me. She's been very patient and understanding with most things so I'd say I have a stronger relationship with her now than I did when I was younger.

With more insight now, how would you tell parents to cope with/try to change difficult behaviours in their ASD children?

I would say don't try to change your children's behaviour because however they behave, they might not be able to help it. Understanding is key and explaining in private when they're in the wrong is helpful. With me, I never viewed my behaviour as wrong so if my mum explained to me, I would eventually understand why I was behaving like I was. Knowing I had Asperger Syndrome definitely helped this.

Is it better to be diagnosed or not?

Absolutely. If you're diagnosed then it's best to accept it and work around it. You can also get all the help you need so it's beneficial to know from a young age.

In what way has autism enhanced your life?

The fact I can write this book is an enhancement... sort of. I'd say the fact it's made me different and in a way unique. The fact that I've learned to deal with the symptoms I feel is an achievement and it's made me into a stronger person in the long run. It didn't enhance my childhood but I'd say it's just starting to enhance my adulthood.

Love you Barry, how does that make you feel?

Very uncomfortable. I could count on a few fingers the amount of people I've ever said it to. The only time I would ever say that and feel comfortable with it being said to me is when I like someone more than just a friend. I feel it's a very intimate thing to say and I don't like it being said if it's not fully meant. I don't like it when someone will say love you to every other person as it makes me feel like another one on the list. I stand by that today. I love you I feel is more intimate than just love you but I accept that others might think differently.

What is the most frustrating thing autism has brought into your life? The biggest challenge?

School. There will never be anything harder for me than school. It was like living a nightmare and I'm glad I got it over with and it's in the past. Everything I struggle with autisically was challenged to the limit at school and I failed a lot before developing a good understanding of myself.

How do autistics understand the feelings of love, when their life is so logical....?

Sometimes it can be hard to differentiate between love and obsession. I don't want to directly talk about something I may view as uncomfortable so I'll talk in third person. Let's say that I had feelings for the same person for a long time, maybe even a few years, then at that stage I'd say its love as obsessions come and go. I think when you can just be yourself without worrying about your traits then that's a sign, when there's no barrier. I think it can be a weakness as it can be very hard to express feelings and others may interpret your behaviour differently to the way you intend it. Also, when things like being touched or feeling awkward socially disappear then I think that's a good indication.

Have you been bullied, teased or felt humiliated because of autism?

Yes although I'd say that I was bullied/teased/humiliated because of my 'strange' behaviour rather than because people knew I had autism. Still, I've had some very unpleasant experiences.

Does your autism make you unhappy or are you happy in your own skin?

It used to make me feel very unhappy, to the point where I overdosed and wanted to end everything. My knowledge that I had limitations doubled with depression was the main trigger for that. Now, I'm proud because it's made me different and although I still have lots of flaws, I'm more confident than I've ever been.

How do you deal with the death of someone as far as we can tell you love?

It's difficult to say because no-one I've ever been very close to has died. I've only ever been close to my mum and that's it. Others have come and gone in phases due to different circumstances. It's very sad of course attending a funeral but I can prepare myself not to cry. If I feel a tear coming on then I can change what I'm thinking about and prevent it.

With your autism... How have you coped with changing of routines due to the M.E.? Or if you have had to stop doing something that helped calm you during a stressful time? My son has ADHD, aspergers and M.E. also. Struggling with routine changes and struggling with things he once enjoyed but can no longer manage.

It's been difficult because M.E. fluctuates day to day which makes it very hard to stick to a routine. I try to leave a bit more leeway with my routines so I can work around setbacks and I set myself smaller tasks. It's taken time to adjust but sticking to a normal routine just isn't possible with M.E.

Do you find changes difficult and how do you manage an ever changing environment?

Yes, absolutely. I find having my 'base' at home which always stays the same helps. It gives me that stability. I spend most of my time at home so there's a lot of stability which helps with environmental changes.

What's the best way for friends to react?

Not to change how they are with you but to treat you like they would anyone else whilst at the same time understanding that it might be a bit harder for you to understand certain things. It helps for them to explain things to you but away from a group so there's not much attention drawn to it.

How do I balance helping my friends to understand Aspergers and my default setting to be private about it? I can see how people miss the old me but it was too hard to maintain the mask. I feel put in a position where I'm counselling them about something I'm still struggling with...

It's tricky. First of all, you should never have to feel that you need to put on a mask in front of your friends. If that means they distance themselves from you than they're not real friends. I've had that happen to me and I have very few friends, leaving it very hard for me to fully trust people. I always have an idea that they'll come and go as that's always been the routine whether I've liked it or not. If your friends want to know more about your condition then maybe you could give them a short leaflet or internet link that will help as I know for us it can be very hard to explain things.

How do you deal with your friends not wanting to know about your Aspergers and M.E.? I get that too with my M.E., friends totally ignore it, even though it's a major part of my life that I struggle with every day.

As harsh as it sounds, if my friends don't want to know about something that's affected me a lot then I have no time for them. As mentioned previously I've lost a lot of friends but I'm more content now than I was previously. Try surrounding yourself with people in a similar position to yourself, maybe a local group or internet forum. They can help if you feel no-one around you wants to listen.

Was it easy to get a job?

I wouldn't say it was easy but I don't think I found it any harder than the average person. I could always come across well in 1 on 1 interviews but if there was something like a group task then I would struggle.

If I ask you to close the door every time because it's draughty... what would you do if someone was behind you?

I would wait for the person behind me to go through the door and then I would close it.

Is sexual intercouse hard?

I'm afraid I'm not the best person to ask as I have always taken celibacy very seriously. Normally, body contact would make me uncomfortable but if I truly loved someone then I doubt it would be much of an issue.

Did you have good or bad reactions from friends and family?

Very few knew but when I started to tell people as I got a bit older, reactions were always a bit awkward and blank so I didn't like to bring it up. I think people felt a bit uncomfortable around me after I'd mentioned it.

What things in your life make you feel happy, secure or content? Is it easy for you to explain these things with autism?

It's not easy as I wouldn't say I was truly happy. I believe I will be in the future but at the moment I'm content with the way things are going. Routine makes me content. Animals make me content. Progress makes me content. Home makes me feel secure.

Would you say that Sheldon on the big bang theory is an accurate picture if having high functioning autism?

I've never seen that show so I can't answer. It's an example though of how little TV I tend to watch as I've explained in a previous chapter.

Do you think the notion that people with autism lack empathy is accurate?

To an extent I do, but it's not because they don't care, it's because expression is very hard. I tried very hard to understand other people's feelings. I touch on this in the school section. I studied through vision watching different sorts of body language and over time I've developed (I hope) a high empathy. I care a lot about certain people and will put myself out for them. It can hurt though when I feel as though I'm putting more effort in than the other person, but I've got used to that.

Are you ever able to relax and completely empty your mind?

I can never fully rest my mind unless I'm exhausted to the extent that I can't stay awake. My mind races but I've worked out certain ways to control that. Reading through forums in bed will help to slowly wind down my mind to the extent that it can't take any more in. It takes the focus away from more real issues that might be bothering me. It's not as bad as it was and I wouldn't say it's something that limits me too much now. It's just slightly inconvenient that I can't fully relax.

Is there anything I/we should be doing to adapt our behaviour/communication to make it easier for someone with autism? Or is normality the best thing?

It's all about equality with maybe a little extra support, with no patronising as I have been very sensitive in the past and still am at times. Treating me normally but with a little extra understanding and careful choice of words as my mind can work very differently to yours. I would say this is the best answer I can give to this question.

How well were you able to interact with other children at school? And now?

I go into much more detail in the social section but in short, not well at all. My mannerisms and social skills were virtually non-existent. Over the years I developed my understanding and I can socialise ok now although groups are still a struggle. 1 on 1 is a lot more comfortable for me.

What is the balance between the assumptions people make due to labels and them being more understanding because of the labels?

I think I'm going down the right route with this... the balance of people being judgemental because of what they've heard and the other is knowing more about the condition because of a label?

Rather than finding a balance, I would say understanding the person's behaviour is key and comparing them to typical behaviours whilst gaining knowledge through basic research of the condition. It's hard because every person is different.

What silly remarks have you heard or have had to deal with?

Take your pick. Lanky used to get to me. 'Baz the spaz' is the reason I prefer to be called by my proper name now. All the usual insults you'd hear knocking around the school playground that I took personally. The thing that I don't like is people treating me a bit simple because they think I'm not as capable as them which is very untrue.

Chapter 15: Coping/Conclusion

Here we are the last chapter... 15, a pretty good number.

As I mentioned in the first chapter, I like to have an introductory chapter and a concluding chapter. Well obviously this is the concluding chapter. I'll talk about ways I've coped with the condition over the years and you'll also see how I cope to this day with certain things. It's also a bit of a summary of what I've already talked about.

Summary

I'm going to start with the 'Diagnosis Process' as that's where it all began. I explained at the start of the 'School Shenanigans' chapter how I came to know about my diagnosis and I'd say I coped fairly well but that was only because I didn't have a great knowledge of what Aspergers was. School has now finished. I was taught not to say anything if I had nothing nice to say so that's probably why I became a quiet person. Being quiet was how I coped; I couldn't cope with being outspoken despite knowing

I was capable in certain situations. At times, I did have fun with friends even if it wasn't as much as I'd have liked, and that helped me to cope better. As you'll have already read, I used to study the way other people interacted and that helped me to prepare for life after school. There are positives if I dig down deep enough. You have to be thick skinned to an extent to get through though and that I wasn't. If I had to give advice to someone then I would say don't be afraid to express yourself but only do it in moderation. Finding that balance I feel is key.

Moving onto the next section 'Work Worries', I'm not the most experienced person in this field so just lock me up in a dark room with a task to do and that's when I'm most effective. Socialising has always been difficult as you know so jobs that follow strict routines suit me better. Having a boss who doesn't understand your condition can be very difficult and on most of my 'first days at work' I've felt like I couldn't cope. Pushing through different tasks whilst trying to switch myself off from the outside world sometimes helped to get me into the mode but it was very hard.

In my opinion, sales is the most uncomfortable field

of work that someone with Aspergers can work in. There are so many things that could go wrong. Having a supervisor is very beneficial as they'll tend to keep a close eye on you and it's always helped me. I've never been too bothered about people being patronising to me as long as they told me what to do. It may be a little different now I'm a bit older though. Working alone suits me a lot as in sorting all my own finances out, making up a business plan and keeping to a routine. The only disadvantage is that sometimes I can feel a little lost without any supervision because I'm not always 100% trusting of my own judgement.

With 'Social Shenanigans' there's so much I could say. It's 1 of my favourite chapters as it gives people a few giggles, then I realise how different I sometimes am. I don't think you'd notice much of a difference if you put a muzzle on me. Dogs don't accept it that well but I'd actually quite like it. As soon as people saw me they'd know I couldn't talk so I wouldn't feel pressurised to do so. I could also probably get away with not shaving for a few days as the muzzle would cover my beard up. On a serious note, being quiet isn't a disadvantage. There is no rule to say you have to be very talkative. Setting a small goal like saying

"Hi" to someone you wouldn't normally speak to each day can give you the self confidence that you do have the ability to mix. Even a smile. It doesn't have to involve talking. Realising all of this has been a good coping strategy for me, apart from the muzzle bit of course. Having a little think and doing a little bit of preparation in your mind before you socialise can put you at ease: it has for me. Making the extra effort at home where you're most comfortable is beneficial even when you don't really feel like it.

Having 'Routine Madness' in my life is a must; it's the routines that help the coping. Prison life would suit me down to the ground actually. Porridge for breakfast at the same time every morning and a visit a day for a set amount of time. Keeping my head down would suit me; it would save me from having to think of conversation. I'd rather sit in a dark room and write up a few tables and statistics. On a serious note, it's best to try and not be too rigid with routine as it's just not sustainable in the long run, you'll wear yourself down. Setting more achievable goals for the smallest of things, even something like always putting your right shoe on 1st, can give you slight satisfaction that you're following a routine. Or checking your e-mails at a certain time can keep things ticking over nicely. Rather than trying to stick to a routine strictly minute by minute, have a bit of leeway with it.

To make life that bit more exciting, having 'Special Interests' can enable you to have that 'alone' time whilst feeling disconnected from society. Really, this covers obsessions though special interests is a kinder way of putting it. They're healthy as long as they're hobbies and not people. The way to know if you have an obsession with a person is if you either declare your love for them after 1 meeting or start sending them over 50 texts a day without reply and get a phone call from the police: if that doesn't occur then you should be Ok. On a serious note, finding interests that don't affect anybody else is key: finding something you can do in your own space that doesn't depend on anyone else. I try to find interests that will help me to progress personally and spiritually.

Early Years Coping

We've had a little summary of the main chapters so now I'm going to share with you how I've coped with the help of others as I haven't really touched up on any of that.

You'll have seen at the end of the 'Diagnosis Process' chapter that I attended a group at the Children's Centre with a few others who were having similar problems to me. I remember at 1st being very nervous but the fact that I was around others who were understanding and non-judgemental meant that I was able to express myself more than I ever could in school. I wanted the group to continue but it was only for 6 weeks. I don't remember vivid details but I do remember it being very helpful to me at the time and I used to look forward to going.

I also attended Church Groups throughout primary school and part of high school which I didn't want to attend at the time but there were positives. I felt more comfortable there than I did at school for a start but there was still the odd individual who would try to spoil things or make you feel worthless. As they say, there always seems to be a class clown lurking about somewhere. The leaders were always good and it was great knowing I could trust them. It helped me socially as I did get on with a fair few of the people and I'd always be glad I'd gone after I'd returned home afterwards. I probably enjoyed it a lot more than I realised thinking back.

I talked about school guidance in the 'School Shenanigans' chapter before and said I would go into more detail later on about the friendship I had with my mentor. He co-ran a Youth Group which, after a lot of persuasion, I attended. He helped me a lot and I even got to go to Macedonia and test out my social skills with people from a different culture. It was great but I was in a dark place at the time meaning I didn't make the most of the experience. It's crazy thinking that it was 8 years ago in 2007 and 8 years before that was 1999 which seems a lifetime away in comparison. The 2 periods of 8 years feel so different. It makes me feel a little sad how time starts to pass more quickly as the years progress, but this is life.

Anyway, The Children's Centre referred me to a new scheme called 'Leisure Inclusions' towards the end of high school and I used to see a lady who would see how I was coping. I got 2 free gym passes and won an award for my commitment to sport but I refused to collect my certificate because it meant going to a ceremony and walking up to the front whilst everyone watched me. I'd rather not have had the award because I was so self-conscious and socially awkward. The lady framed the certificate and brought it round to the house, it remains on my bedroom wall to this day.

I mentioned previously in the 'Q + A' chapter that I once overdosed. After being in hospital for a week I was referred to a Crisis Prevention Team whilst regularly seeing a psychiatrist. I really didn't like the idea of seeing this team and wasn't keen at all after their 1st visit to the house. Nothing went wrong but the guy I saw was a little too flamboyant for me which was fine but it meant it would draw attention to me if I went out with him. I actually grew to really like him and we went out for coffee and also played snooker which I enjoyed. The idea was to get me out of the house for a bit each week and try to get me to socialise. I saw a woman from a different team for coffee a few times too. It all helped and the guy thought I'd benefit from joining a Drama group. The reason I've mentioned the overdose is because I feel strongly that the main reason I did it was due to feeling so worthless and limited due to having Asperger Syndrome. I couldn't cope knowing it wasn't an illness and that I was never going to 'recover' from it.

I saw many different psychiatrists and psychologists and this helped me at times. I actually preferred talking to them rather than acquaintances at college. It was more formal and I was asked inoffensive questions and this suited me. It was professional and although I felt more depressed after I'd been to appointments, (which defeated the object of going) it was still good to talk to someone. I felt a sense of satisfaction when they were writing notes. It made me think we were going somewhere and they would magically tell me something I didn't already know. It never happened.

I mentioned just before about attending a Drama group. I went there for a few months in the hope that it would do my confidence the world of good yet it was 1 of the most uncomfortable things I've ever done. It was meant to give me confidence and help me with socialising but it made me even more nervous. Acting was so unnatural to me that I did my best to avoid being picked out to do anything. I soon found out I was going to perform in a Christmas play which was just a few weeks away. The worry took over my whole life for those few weeks and I did the cowardly thing by getting my mum to ring up the group and tell them I was ill. I never went back after that. Attending the group had the opposite effect on me to what had been hoped for. Pushing yourself isn't always a positive thing as this experience taught me. I gave it a go but it just wasn't my thing.

At the same time as this I was still seeing the usual lady from Leisure Inclusions and then a very tall athletic man joined her for 1 visit. He said he'd like to act as my personal trainer. He was a very fit runner who'd taken part in many marathons. He was 6'4 and you'll know by now what I'm like with heights. I was in my element. I wasn't used to hanging out with someone taller than me. He even took me to coffee shops and introduced me to the cinnamon latte. Unfortunately, it was only for a limited period of time, but we'd become friends and so he arranged to see me out of work hours. We went on a mountain bike ride in Wales which I was really looking forward to. He gave me more confidence in myself and I felt I could tell him about certain problems I was having without the risk of information being passed on to anyone else. The bike ride was a disaster though and I fell shoulder first into a ditch. I had heavy bags to carry but he made me get the train home, despite having a car, which upset me as I was struggling. My shoulder wasn't right for years after that. Contact began to dwindle and he disappeared off the face of the earth very shortly after. He didn't reply to calls or texts and I had no way of contacting him. It always took me a long time to learn to trust a person so it was very hurtful when this happened. He was great at the time but I didn't appreciate the way I was treated towards the end of our friendship. I was pushed into doing water sports with kids younger than me and only agreed to do it because he said he'd join in which he didn't. He even forced me into giving a waitress his phone number after we'd eaten out which surely wasn't right given my social problems. Looking back, I saw small signs when I volunteered to help him with a University project. I had to go in twice because he lost the work the 1st time round but the 2nd time he was very 'cool' with me for no apparent reason. Still to this day I don't understand it but back then I dwelled on it for quite a while.

The reason I've shared all of this is that sometimes I used to feel that everyone who did good for me could do no wrong. I tended to put people on a pedestal. This was a harsh lesson that people are not always what they seem. I came out of that friendship feeling I was the more level headed person of us 2 when it should have been the other way around.

Other Coping Mechanisms

Lastly, I'm going to conclude other coping mechanisms that continue to help me throughout life. These are things that I haven't talked much about in the rest of the book.

The biggest coping mechanism for me is religion. Being a Christian has given me the motivation and courage to keep going in the bad times. Without it I would probably have attempted to take my own life again long before now when I was in a dark place.

I know that people are entitled to their own beliefs and I have no problem with that, but I don't understand why some people will claim to be a believer yet disregard certain things that are in black and white. It's not for me to judge but as I mentioned before, some things are black and white and I find it hard understanding why people don't follow certain things. It helps me with the lack of social interaction, I can pray whenever I want and I won't be told to shut up. Doing a daily reading in the morning is part of my routine and that gives me a sense of satisfaction. I feel that if it weren't for my faith I wouldn't be here today, I wouldn't see the point. It may sound a little controversial but that's my opinion. That's how much it means to me. What I don't like is when people will try to catch me out full well knowing I have a problem with getting my words out. I don't like big long words; if something can be simplified then why not do it? I don't find it impressive at all.

1 thing I don't like is debating. I'm confident enough in my faith to avoid getting into meaningless discussions where others will try and put you down. I don't force my beliefs on anyone so it's only fair that others don't force their views onto me either.

I've talked about how fitness helps me so I won't mention that again. The other thing that I would say really helps me to cope with life and keep level-headed is realism.

Being realistic can sometimes be seen as being pessimistic but I disagree with that. I rarely feel let down because I don't set my expectations high. What

I will do is do the best I think I can, these days anyway. I'm a lot more motivated than when I was back in school.

I don't like summer because it's too relaxed. Being too relaxed means there's more time to dwell on things. I think of people enjoying themselves with their partners or families and it makes me feel sad because I've never really had that. I imagine couples on a hot beach with their beach bodies having a nice time splashing each other with water and running through the sand. I would think of someone I like and imagined doing the same but I didn't like it because it would likely never become a reality. I only like to think of things that will become a reality. I'm very realistic. If it's not realistic then I don't want to know. I don't like the idea of karaoke. I only want to sing in public if there's a chance I could sing on stage. Karaoke might be called a laugh but it's not really funny if you're singing out of tune and people are laughing at you. That's my nightmare. I want people to clap me, not laugh at me. It's a sense of achievement that it's been worthwhile. I didn't set out in life to be laughed at. Comedians do, but I don't... unless it's laughing with me of course.

I don't like looking back at old photographs either because I don't want to look back at the past. What if I came across a photo taken with someone that I really liked who was no longer in my life? It would make me upset so I'd rather not see it. I don't like how I look in old photographs and don't like 'reliving the memories' because it was in the past and it might not ever happen again. I don't like that.

I don't see the above as being miserable, it's realism for me. It keeps me level-headed and I think that's the best way for me.

I hope that this book has been helpful and interesting to read. If I mentioned absolutely everything then I'd be writing for ever but I'd like to think I've got the main points across and have presented them in a way that people will understand.

Thank you for reading... "Life Is Complicated"! (1st exclamation mark in this book).